School
To
Work
To
Success

School To Work To Success

A Practical Guide to Finding a Rewarding Career and Enjoying Life

by

DALE G. CALDWELL

5th Printing 2015
Available in E-Book 2010

© 2008 Dale G. Caldwell
All rights reserved.

Published by Luminary Media Group,
an imprint of Pine Orchard, Inc.
www.pineorchard.com

Printed in USA

ISBN-10 1-930580-76-2
ISBN-13 978-1930580-76-3

Library of Congress Control Number: 2008908093

DEDICATION

This book is dedicated to my mother, Grace Estelle Dungee Caldwell; my father, Reverend Gilbert Haven Caldwell, Jr.; my brother, Paul Douglass Caldwell; my wife, Sharon Marie Caldwell; and my daughter Ashley Marie Caldwell.

They have been, and will always be, the foundation of my spiritual, mental, and physical health.

Table of Contents

ACKNOWLEDGMENTS

I have learned a great deal from the many wonderful family members, friends, co-workers, and bosses who have entered my life over the years. It has been a blessing to interact with so many outstanding people in very different personal and work environments.

I have also had the good fortune of holding both junior and senior positions in the public, private, and civic sectors. This book is based on my successes and failures as a student, new employee, human resources executive, management consultant, nonprofit leader, government official, financial planner, and senior executive. Each chapter of this book is a compilation of the many lessons I have learned through this journey.

I will never be able to thank everyone who has taught me important life and career lessons over the years. However, I acknowledge just a few of these people who have played an important role in my career in the paragraphs below:

I must begin these acknowledgments by thanking my wife Sharon and daughter Ashley for their support in the development of this book. Their love and guidance helped to make this book possible.

I am grateful to my wonderful parents Reverend Gilbert (a retired United Methodist minister) and Grace Caldwell (a retired schoolteacher). They were both extremely accomplished in their respective careers. However, they did not know a great deal about the keys to success in careers outside their own. Nevertheless, they provided the incredible support and guidance that I needed to pursue senior level careers in the public, private, and civic sectors.

I also owe my brother Paul, who has been a successful engineer with several of the largest aerospace engineering companies in the world, a great deal of thanks. Early in my life, I made the erroneous assumption that everyone wanted to manage people. Paul has taught me that many people are as passionate about non-managerial technical positions as others are about senior management positions.

I am fortunate that my boss at Quaker Oats (my first full-time job after college) taught me early in my career that success in the world of work is not based on merit. In addition, I owe my co-workers at the Wharton Small Business Development Center (SBDC) a debt of gratitude for inspiring me to spend much of my professional life as a management consultant.

I am grateful to all my bosses and co-workers at Deloitte Consulting who helped me develop my analytical skills and taught me how to work hard and smart. I extend a special thanks to my first and last management consulting boss Ed Ruzinsky who has had a legendary career in multiple businesses. His incredibly calm and positive approach to the stress of business has been a great inspiration. I owe a professional debt to Marc Schwarz who took a chance on hiring me when I was a young inexperienced Wharton MBA student. Marc's intense focus on business and willingness to make me uncomfortable helped to push me to get the most out of my professional skills.

I am beholden to my former boss John DiMaggio for making consulting fun and sponsoring many of my promotions and raises over the years. I am also thankful that I had the great pleasure of working with Jim Wall, Paul Gallagher, and Jack Beighley. These outstanding human resources professionals taught me how to recruit, train, and develop employees. I am especially grateful to Tim Washington and Dexter Bridgeman for partnering with me in the development of some very successful career and life mentoring programs that have helped young people in many countries around the world.

I am thankful to the entire board of the Newark Alliance for hiring me to be the first Executive Director. I am particularly grateful to my bosses: former New Jersey Governor Thomas H. Kean for teaching me how important compassionate leadership is to success; Philanthropist Ray Chambers for teaching me how important mental and physical health is to impactful leadership; and Prudential Financial CEO Art Ryan for demonstrating that you can be an incredibly successful corporate CEO and have a passionate interest in helping local communities at the same time.

I owe a debt of gratitude to former New Jersey Department of Community Affairs (DCA) Commissioner Susan Bass Levin for teaching me that the key to success in the public sector is being honest and working harder than anyone else. I also owe a debt of gratitude to George Lumsby and Terry McCarthy who taught me how top-notch executive recruiters identify candidates.

Finally, I am thankful to Heather Allen, Ethel Winckler, and Suzanne Winderman for their efforts to make me successful over the years. I am more grateful than they will ever know for their guidance and support through many challenging aspects of my career.

FOREWORD

by Matt Stevens

Welcome to the Real World!

If you have not heard this phrase yet, you will hear it soon. It will come from your parents, relatives, and authority figures such as teachers, coaches, and employers. This phrase is an indication that you are growing into a respected citizen and a soon-to-be employee.

The *Real World* can be a fun and enjoyable place if you set high expectations. It can also, unfortunately, be a place that you despise. Do you know anyone who wakes up each day and literally hates to go to work? In most cases, people like that did not properly prepare for their job; and as a result, they choose to work at a place that is not fulfilling. Conversely, do you know anyone who wakes up each day and loves to go to work? Those people most likely took time to ask themselves, "*What do I want to do with my life?*"

Once you ask and answer that question, you are on the road to being a person who loves to wake up each morning and go to work. Isn't that the person you want to be?

Your first job can be a rewarding experience if you understand why you are working. In most cases, people obtain employment because they desire to earn money. If you are a high school or college student, you probably want a job to earn money to purchase the newest video game system, save money to go toward your class prom, or simply have spending cash in your pocket. All of these are good reasons to want a job; however, I suggest that you seriously consider obtaining a job where you can do something that you enjoy.

Imagine someone paying you to do something that you like to do! This can be a reality if you take the time to explore opportunities that match your interest. If you like cooking and dealing with the public, then a job at a fast-food restaurant and a career in the food industry may be ideal for you. If you enjoy listening to music and talking to other people about it, a job at a music store and a career in the arts might be your "cup of tea." In any case, you have an opportunity to choose where it is that you want to work.

This insightful, well-written book will provide you with the secrets of succeeding in work and life. By reading it and reflecting on each chapter, you will start down the road to the *Real World*.

Good luck!

Matt Stevens
President & CEO
Empower Today's Youth

INTRODUCTION

Exposure Is the Key

The foundation of success in life is a satisfying career. Unfortunately, most people do not find the right career because they are focused on working for money instead of pursuing a profession that they enjoy. Webster's dictionary defines *career* as "an occupation or profession followed as a life's work." The dictionary defines *job* as "something that has to get done." The people who make an effort to find a profession that can become "a life's work" are much more likely to have a satisfying career and life than those who take a job because it is "something they have to do." All too often people take the first job that they can find without thinking about their skills, interests, and career aspirations. They may be able to pay their bills; however, they are frequently miserable at work and at home.

I have had the opportunity to help a lot of high school and college students find jobs and learn about career opportunities. As a former human resources executive and recruiter for several major corporations, I taught students and adults how to identify job opportunities, develop an effective resume, enhance their interview skills, and succeed at work. As a former Certified Financial Planner (CFP), I helped students and adults manage their money and effectively plan for their financial future.

One of the things that I learned over the years is that many students are expected to aspire to careers that they do not know about. I therefore created a program called "*Take Your Community To Work Day*" in which students had a chance to visit local corporations in 80 cities in the United States and 11 other countries. I also established a program called "*Classroom Press Conference*" where executives from corporations, government agencies, and nonprofit organizations were interviewed by students in classrooms in urban communities. These programs effectively exposed students to career opportunities they otherwise would not know about. They also taught students how to find a job and succeed in the world of work. More importantly, through those programs I discovered how to help students find jobs and careers.

This book reflects the many things I have learned about employment, finance, and life over the years. I have found that lists are the best way to communicate information that is difficult to comprehend. Therefore, to ensure that the lessons in this book are easy to understand, I have grouped the information of each chapter into lists of five or ten. In addition, to enhance the effectiveness of the book, I have included a useful exercise in the recommendation section of each chapter. The book is designed to serve as a resource for a reader's entire life. Some of the chapters will be extremely useful to readers immediately while other chapters will be helpful at a later date. Each chapter was written to stand alone so that it will be easier to review chapters in the order that is most useful to the reader.

The Five Rules of Professional and Life Success

It is very easy for students in high school and college to look for a *job* instead of a *career*. Frequently, students will take any job they can get so they have spending money. Unfortunately, most of these jobs lead to disappointment because they rarely transition into a career. Some students holding these jobs make excuses about their inability to get a better job. They claim that they will never have a chance to get a good job because their life has been so difficult. They believe that other young people (because the "others" are perceived as rich, smart, good-looking, etc.) will get all the good jobs. They therefore make little or no effort to find a better job or pursue a career.

These disillusioned students have the mistaken perception that success for some people is easy; however, *success is not easy for anyone.*

The first step in pursuing a job and finding the right career is accepting the Five Rules of Professional and Life Success. If you are a student interested in succeeding at work and life, you should strive to remember the five rules listed below:

1. Life is tough.
2. Life is unfair.
3. Success only comes from hard work.
4. There is no excuse for not working hard.
5. Treat people the way that you want to be treated.

1. Life Is Tough

No one can guarantee that you will find a satisfying career. However, if you accept these five rules, you will be better prepared to find an appropriate career. Unfortunately, many people do not accept these rules. They watch the unrealistic depiction of life on television and think that life should be easy. *Life is not easy.*

Contrary to what people might believe, all people, regardless of their wealth or life circumstances, have to deal with life challenges. For example, the teenage years are difficult for people living in rich and poor households. The emotional, intellectual, and physical obstacles that teenagers experience are common for everyone, regardless of their socio-economic circumstances. The temptation to drink alcohol or take drugs is found throughout all communities. All too frequently, the stress of school, a job, family, and life can discourage students from trying because they think that their situation is uniquely hopeless. They mistakenly believe that life is only hard for them. To be successful at work and life, you must accept the fact that most other people face the same obstacles that you face. Consequently, there is no excuse for you not to do whatever it takes to succeed. *Life is tough for everyone.*

2. Life Is Unfair

Many people think that everyone has an equal chance to succeed in society. The reality is that some people have a better chance of success than others. *Life is not fair.*

The saying "success in life comes from being at the right place at the right time" is very true. Every story of success that I have ever heard was based on someone being in the right place at the right time. This is true for a great job, a great relationship, or a great house. Unfortunately, the uneven distribution of this "being in the right place at the right time" phenomenon gives people the inaccurate belief that success is impossible for them.

Life is unfair because most people are not prepared to succeed — even if success is knocking on their door. The saying "success is where opportunity meets preparation" is very accurate. Everyone, no matter what his or her circumstances are, has many great opportunities in life.

Unfortunately, most people are not prepared to take advantage of these opportunities. They are not prepared for an interview when the right job comes along. They are not ready to settle down when the right potential husband or wife comes along. They have not managed their finances correctly when the right house comes on the market. The objective of this book is to make sure that readers are prepared for the right employment and financial opportunity when it comes along. (I'm not offering any relationship advice. You will have to handle that on your own. ☺)

3. *Success Only Comes from Hard Work*

Many people think that success is easy. However, achieving success is not easy because it only comes from hard work. All successful people have worked harder than others to achieve their success. One of the most psychologically devastating myths is that success is easy for some people. Movie stars get paid a lot of money and receive many benefits that come with their fame. Star athletes get incredible financial contracts and a lot of time off. Lottery winners receive millions of dollars for buying a cheap lottery ticket. Corporate chief executive officers (CEOs) and company presidents become billionaires for creating products that are purchased by consumers. At a superficial level, the lives of these individuals seem perfect and easy. However, if you would take time to understand how much hard work was required, not only to achieve their success but to keep it, you would understand the importance of hard work and persistence.

Movie stars frequently wait tables and act for free for years before they get their first major acting break. They typically spend a lot of money and time perfecting their acting skills. The best athletes spend hours each day working on their bodies to give them an advantage over other athletes who are not willing to work equally as hard. Lottery winners typically buy lottery tickets for many years before winning a big payout. However, they must work extremely hard on financial and life planning to keep the money. Many people believe that there is a curse on lottery winners because a surprisingly large number of them (who do not work hard on keeping their money) go bankrupt after winning millions of dollars. Corporate CEOs deal with unimaginable stress at work and at home on a daily basis. They are also forced to work a majority of the 168 hours available each week.

Success only comes from hard work and an incredible passion to succeed. To be successful, you must be committed to working as hard as you possibly can to achieve a career and life goal.

4. *There Is No Excuse for Not Working Hard*

Some people think that their particular circumstances prevent them from working hard. No matter how poor, sick, or uneducated people are, they can work hard enough to succeed if they want to. There is no reason not to work hard enough to succeed. Human beings are naturally prone to excuses. If something goes wrong, it is human nature to blame someone or something else. However, we control our own destiny. Every successful movie star, athlete, lottery winner, and corporate CEO faced obstacles that may have seemed insurmountable to some people. However, they were able to overcome these obstacles and succeed.

Many of these people succeed in spite of facing circumstances more challenging than those faced by the students and adults reading this book. If they can work hard enough to succeed, then you can work hard enough to succeed.

5.   *Treat People the Way You Want To Be Treated*

Many people believe that working hard is enough. *Working hard is not enough.*

In addition to hard work, success comes from treating people the way that you want to be treated. By doing this, you will be able to interact effectively with people at work and at home. The world is run by people; it is therefore extremely important that you know how to effectively interact with people.

The saying "the higher you rise, the harder you fall" is very true. It is amazing how many people achieve success and forget that their success is due to the support of many people. There is a tendency for people to believe that because they have been successful, they do not owe anything to anyone. They therefore treat people very differently than they want to be treated. They are selfish, abusive, domineering, controlling, condescending, and/or rude to their co-workers, friends, and family. This almost always catches up to them. They convince themselves that rules only apply to the "little people" so they violate rules, regulations, and laws. All too often, the people to whom they have been disrespectful expose their violations. As a result, these successful people lose their fame, fortune, and power and are frequently disgraced for the rest of their life.

Treating people the way you want to be treated is an essential secret to achieving success in life. By treating people with the same respect you think that you deserve, you will have more friends and you will be exposed to more career and personal opportunities. Best of all, your outlook toward life will be much more positive; and you will attract more employment opportunities and have more successful relationships. Clearly, if you follow the Five Rules of Professional and Life Success, you will be much more likely to have a positive attitude and succeed in both your career and life.

Book Overview

Most students in high school and college have no idea what a good job is, how to get it, or why getting a job is important. Unfortunately, because the world of work has changed so much, parents and teachers often do not know how to help students develop a job-search strategy that is appropriate for today's marketplace. To make matters worse, there is a shortage of information on the specific skills necessary for success at work. It is also very hard to find the unique advice that high school and first- and second-year college students need to find summer jobs, internships, part-time and full-time positions that lay the foundation for a successful career. In addition, there is no effective guide to financial planning for high school and college students.

This book was written to fill the school-to-work information void. The book is divided into three sections: Section I provides clear answers to questions that students have about finding a job. Section II provides advice on ways that students and full-time employees can succeed at work. Finally, Section III answers students' questions about managing both their money and their life.

SECTION I

Finding a Job

CHAPTER 1

Why Do I Need A Job?

Ten Reasons To Find a Job

A job is simply an activity where a person works on a regular basis for an organization (corporate, government, or nonprofit). There are many volunteer jobs (like internships) where people work to gain experience, not to get paid. However, most jobs provide payments (paychecks) to workers for their services. A paycheck is an agreed-upon payment that people receive from the business they are working for in exchange for their time and effort in completing the work requested. The definition of a job and paycheck may be obvious to some people. However, amazingly, many people do not take time to fully understand the benefits of a job (other than the income that it generates).

Students in high school and college frequently look at a job as simply a vehicle to help them put more spending money in their pocket. They do not take time to think about the many other opportunities that a job provides. In addition, they assume that finding and keeping a job is easy. They therefore do not put in the effort necessary to find a job that will provide maximum benefits to their life at home and in school. To make matters worse, they are usually not willing to do whatever is necessary to succeed in the job that they have. Consequently, students frequently have trouble finding and keeping a job.

There are many reasons that finding a job is important for everyone of working age. However, there are ten major reasons for college and high school students to find a job. These are to:

1. Make money.
2. Get business experience.
3. Learn work skills.
4. Make business contacts.
5. Become a better student.
6. Learn how to deal with the challenges of work.
7. Learn time management.
8. Make new friends at work.
9. Learn how to manage money.
10. Get a better idea of what career to pursue.

---

1. To Make Money

The first, and most common, reason to find a job is to make money. Students are constantly complaining that they do not have enough money to buy the things they need and want. They frequently expect their parents to provide money. The money that they receive from their parents is almost never enough. They therefore either do without the things they want or borrow money from others to get those things. Obviously, borrowing money can lead to a lot of financial and personal problems so that is never a good option. Clearly, the best option for making money is to find a job that pays well. Unfortunately, finding the right job takes a great deal of hard work and preparation.

---

2. To Get Business Experience

There is no substitute for having a job while you are a student. The business experience that you receive from having a job when you are young is invaluable. Many people with successful careers say that their work experience as students put them on the right career path. Their jobs either taught them that they were passionate about a certain career or that they hated a certain job and never wanted to work in that position again. The experience gained from a job includes learning:

a) How to deal with the unique pressures and requirements of work.
b) What you need to know and do when you have a job.
c) How to manage your time and interact with others.
d) What job opportunities and career options there are.
e) How an organization works.

This information is essential no matter what you want to do after you graduate from high school and/or college.

---

3. To Learn Work Skills

It is one thing to get business experience from a job. It is a completely different thing to learn work skills. There are many skills that you need to be a successful student. Unfortunately, the world of work requires many different skills that are not easily learned at school. Of course, different jobs teach different skills. However, the top 5 work skills that most students learn when they have a job include how to:

a) Wear the appropriate clothes, behave professionally, and arrive on time.
b) Effectively communicate with other people at work.
c) Complete a work assignment on time (or even early).
d) Utilize word processing and financial software successfully.
e) Work as a contributing member of a business team.

These work skills are the foundation of success in a job or career. Unfortunately, many students have trouble in their first job because they do not do one or more of these things effectively. However, the motivated students usually learn what they need to know in their next job.

---

4. To Make Business Contacts

Most people know the saying that "success in business comes from who you know, not what you know." This saying is obviously an exaggeration. However, there is a great deal of truth in its premise. All too often great job opportunities come from friends of friends or people that you interact with at work or in the community. What is not mentioned in the saying is that success only comes to those who work hard. Many students find that if they do an exceptional job at work, they are exposed to more career opportunities than average workers. One of the secrets of work is that doing well at a job (no matter what job you have) will expose you to important business contacts that can lead to lucrative business opportunities.

5. *To Become a Better Student*

One of the biggest myths in school is that getting good grades comes from being smart. The key to good grades in school is not intelligence. It is discipline. The students who make an effort to study on a regular basis and fully comprehend what they are learning are the students who get good grades and go to the best colleges. Unfortunately, many of the smartest students in class do not get good grades because they are not willing to focus on their school work. One of the biggest benefits of a job for students is that it teaches them discipline. In school, you can often get away with being late, not doing your class work, or "playing the fool in school." You cannot do this at work. You have to show up on time or you will be fired. You have to do your work as requested or you will be fired. You have to behave in an appropriate way or you will be fired. Of course, when you are fired, you will not get the money that motivated you to get the job in the first place. It is amazing how students who have no discipline in school develop incredible discipline at work because a paycheck is at stake. Best of all, many students do much better at school because they apply the discipline that they learn at work to school.

6. *To Learn How To Deal with the Challenges of Work*

Getting to school on time, taking tests, answering questions in class, and doing homework are often challenging. However, the demands of work present very different types of challenges. Fortunately, students who meet the challenges of work will be well prepared for success in school and life. The five major challenges that students will learn to deal with at work are:

a) Getting to work on time.
b) Managing the expectations of other people.
c) Following orders.
d) Working late.
e) Accepting criticism.

Getting To Work on Time

If you are working for a paycheck, there is no excuse for not showing up to work on time. Your boss expects you to show up to work when you are scheduled to be there. The toughest thing about work for many students is getting to work on time. However, getting to work on time is the first lesson of personal responsibility. When you accept a job, you are guaranteeing that you will show up on time and do the best you can at work. Students that are effectively able to meet this challenge are likely to be successful employees. Unfortunately, those who are frequently late to work will be fired.

Managing the Expectations of Other People

The objective of every employee should be to exceed the expectations of other people (especially the expectations of their boss). The natural tendency of most workers is to promise more than they can deliver. Typically, people will tell their boss that they can finish a report in three days, even though they know that it will probably take four days to complete. Experienced employees will promise that the report will be completed in five days, even though they know they can probably finish it in four days. If both employees finish the report in four days, the employee who promised the report in five days will be praised because he or she exceeded the expectations of their boss while the employee who promised the report in three days will be criticized because the expectations of their boss were not met.

Following Orders

As an employee of an organization, students will be given many instructions that will require them to take an action immediately. Unfortunately, most students have not developed the ability to listen in great detail. They are used to listening to music or watching television while they receive instruction from others. However, the world of work does not allow for casual listening. Instead, workers are required to listen intently to specific orders from their boss and act on them accordingly. Students who develop the ability to effectively listen to orders and carry them out will be extremely successful at work.

Working Late

Corporations are focused on making a profit from the provision of goods and/or services on a timely basis. Government is dedicated to delivering services needed by citizens. Nonprofits are designed to meet the needs of the communities that they are attempting to serve. Students working in corporations, government agencies, or nonprofit organizations will all be faced with many work deadlines. They will be forced to work as long as needed to complete a work assignment on time. This means that they may have to stay later than anticipated at work. This is extremely difficult when it first happens. However, students will soon learn that it is a necessary part of a job in today's world of work.

Accepting Criticism

Probably the biggest challenge that every worker faces is accepting criticism. It is very difficult to hear your boss or co-worker tell you that you are not good at something or that you need to improve your skills. However, the only way to grow as a person and a worker is to find out what you need to work on to be more effective. Some people need to learn how to use the computer more effectively while others need to enhance their verbal and written communication skills. Others need to learn how to complete assignments on time. It is very easy to get angry when someone tells you that you need to get better at something. However, if you put your pride aside and hear them out, chances are they have some very helpful information that will make you a better employee.

---

7. *To Learn Time Management*

Time management is one of the keys to success at work and in life. Most people think that money is the most valuable thing in the world. However, in reality, time is much more valuable than money because if you are out of time in life, money is worthless. However, if you have time, you can make money. Unfortunately, most students have no idea how to effectively manage their time. They wake up late, go to bed late, waste time, and do what they want to do whenever it is convenient. When they are working, they realize that they have to learn to manage their time before, during, and after work. They have to get up early enough to allow them to get into work on time. They have to manage their time at work in a way that allows them to complete everything that they are supposed to complete. They have to schedule their time after work in a manner that will ensure that they are adequately prepared for the demands of work the next day. This often means that they cannot afford to waste time. Effective time management will make you happier because you will be more productive and have greater control over your life.

---

8. *To Make New Friends at Work*

A surprise benefit of working for many students is the number of friendships that they develop at work. There is an assumption on many students' part that they can only relate to their classmates at school. However, most companies hire student workers and recent graduates because they are trying to identify good long-term employees. Many companies encourage social activity among employees to improve their effectiveness at work. One of the best things about the world of work is the diversity of skills and backgrounds of employees in most companies. Student workers will frequently get a chance to meet people from countries and communities that they otherwise would never meet. The most successful employees are those who can work effectively with people of different racial, gender, experiential, and skill backgrounds. The friendships that students make at work often last a lifetime and lead to many future career opportunities.

9. To Learn How To Manage Money

When students start their first job, all they think about is the money that they will make when they receive their first paycheck. They rarely think about how they will manage their money once they receive it. One of the best lessons that students learn from working is how to effectively manage the money they receive. Many people believe that you should only think about managing money if you have a lot of it. However, the truth is that everyone who makes money should think about managing it. One helpful exercise for students is to record every penny that they spend for three months (whether it is for a stick of gum or the purchase of books). When students do this, they discover that they have more money to manage than they thought (because they waste so much money on non-essential items). They therefore should spend less on extraneous items and put money in the bank, savings bonds, or mutual funds. This is an excellent way for students to find enough money on a tight budget to begin the process of investing.

10. To Get a Better Idea of What Career To Pursue

Most people believe that there is no relationship between their first job and their career. However, this should not be the case. A student's first job has the potential to provide valuable information about their career options. In addition, a student's subsequent jobs should be chosen to provide information about potential careers. Ideally, students should write down a list of careers that they are potentially interested in pursuing. Once they put this list together, they should pursue jobs that are somewhat related to one or more of these careers. The jobs that they accept should help them narrow down their career interests.

RECOMMENDATION

There are many reasons why most students should get a job as soon as they reach working age. The ten reasons listed in this chapter clearly indicate why students need a job. These reasons should be sufficient motivation for you to do the research necessary to find a job of interest. You should also be inspired to learn more about potential careers. The sooner you start a job and career search, the better. To help you target your job search, you should complete the ranking on the next page.

RANKING OF REASONS TO FIND A JOB

You may not agree with the priority ranking of the ten reasons to get a job in this chapter. You should therefore rank the ten reasons to find a job (1-10) in order of importance to you (1 being most important) below:

A. ____To Make Money

B. ____To Get Business Experience

C. ____To Learn Work Skills

D. ____To Make Business Contacts

E. ____To Become a Better Student

F. ____To Learn How To Deal with the Challenges of Work

G. ____To Learn To Manage Time

H. ____To Make New Friends

I. ____To Learn How To Manage Money

J. ____To Get a Better Idea of What Career to Pursue

By completing this ranking, you will develop a deeper understanding of the most important reasons you have for getting a job. The preferences that you identify in this ranking should help you focus your job search on securing positions that have the elements that are most important to you.

CHAPTER 2

Can School Really Prepare Me for a Job?

The Value of School

Most students do not understand that what they learn in school can help them succeed at work. Clearly, the ability to read and comprehend what you are reading is a necessary business skill that you should learn at school. The ability to communicate effectively both verbally and in writing is often the difference between success and failure at work. These skills are also taught at school. There are many business-related skills that you learn at school. If you are a student and you take school seriously, you will learn many important work-related skills in class. However, the ten most important business skills that you learn at school are:

1. Verbal communication skills
2. Reading comprehension skills
3. Written communication skills
4. Self-discipline
5. Problem-solving skills
6. Test-taking skills
7. Completing an assignment on time
8. Interacting with different people
9. Teamwork
10. Computer skills

A brief description of each of these skills is provided on the next few pages.

1. Verbal Communication Skills

The ability to speak clearly and convey your point of view in a concise manner is the single most important work skill. If you are not able to effectively communicate with your co-workers, you will not succeed at work. People will find it difficult to work with you if they don't know what you are saying. How you speak is often as important as what you say. Using slang words or grammatically incorrect sentences gives the impression that you do not take your job seriously. You would never think of wearing a bathing suit to an office. Obviously, a bathing suit is much too casual for a place of work. Likewise, using casual speech at work is not appropriate. It is also important for you to listen carefully, analyze what you have heard, and give clear and concise answers to questions. All too often employees will respond to questions with the very first response that comes to mind. This frequently leads to misstatements at work that can jeopardize their employment. Some people find that taking a few seconds to think about what they want to say before they speak is an effective way to successfully communicate at work. If you learn to take this pause with co-workers, it will allow you to collect your thoughts and provide insightful answers. The more insightful comments you make at work, the more successful you will be in your job.

2. Reading Comprehension Skills

The ability to read and understand what you are reading is an essential work skill learned at school. No matter what job you have, reading will be involved. You may have to read instruction manuals, rules, regulations, employment policies, or standard work memorandums. If you cannot read very well, you will not be successful at work because you will not be able to understand critical information related to your job. School teaches students the reading skills they need to be successful at work. The ability to understand what you read is called reading comprehension. Unfortunately, many people who can read do not have strong reading comprehension skills. They can read the words but have trouble understanding the full meaning of what they are reading. One of the major objectives of both high school and college is to teach students how to understand what they read (no matter how complex it is). Students who are serious about succeeding at work will make an effort to do well in courses that teach reading comprehension. Many students think that math, science, and English courses have no value for them if they are not going into these fields. However, these courses are extremely effective at teaching students reading comprehension and problem-solving skills. Clearly, the ability to understand what you read at work is an important skill learned at school.

3. Written Communication Skills

Many employees have excellent verbal communication and reading comprehension skills. However, they do not excel at work because they have poor writing skills. They cannot effectively communicate their ideas on paper. They are therefore passed over for promotion or even fired. Unfortunately, many students do not understand how important strong writing skills are to success at work. On a daily basis, employees are required to write emails, respond to emails, write letters, and compose business memorandums (memos). Consequently, it becomes very obvious which employees write well and which ones do not write well. School is the best place to learn writing skills. Students who want to succeed at work will make an effort to excel at assignments that require writing. School papers and book reports help students develop the writing skills needed for business. Business writing is a little different than the writing required in schools. However, the writing learned in school serves as an outstanding foundation for business writing.

4. Self-Discipline

The employees that have the most self-discipline are usually the most successful. A job presents you with many challenges that require strong self-discipline to complete. Many work assignments will force you to learn new subjects and work at an uncomfortably fast pace. The only effective way to address these challenging assignments is to discipline yourself to develop a structured, orderly work approach. The self-discipline that you need to succeed at work is similar to the self-discipline you need to succeed at school. Completing homework assignments, preparing for tests, even successfully participating in a sport or club require self-discipline.

Effective self-discipline leads to a strong work ethic that includes daily activities designed to enhance your ability to succeed. In most instances, your success in school, a sport, or a club is directly related to the self-discipline you demonstrate. If you are able to develop discipline in school, you should be able to develop the self-discipline needed to succeed at work.

5. Problem-Solving Skills

The ability to develop solutions to problems is an extremely important business skill. Math, science, and English courses help to teach both reading comprehension and problem-solving skills. They help students break problems down into their component parts. Once identified and analyzed, students learn how to solve the problems related to each component part. Students are then able to combine the solutions related to the component parts of the problem and successfully solve the problem as a whole. The problems that students face at work are very different than the problems they face at school. However, the skill of breaking down problems into their component parts at school is an excellent foundation for developing important problem-solving skills at work.

6. Test-Taking Skills

Very few people like taking tests at school or understand the important lessons learned by taking tests. However, tests help students develop important business skills. Tests teach students how to:

a) **Prepare for tests.**
b) **Answer questions under pressure.**
c) **Accept criticism.**

Prepare for Tests

Frequently, students have no idea what material will be on a test so they have to study all the information learned in class. They therefore learn how to process large amounts of information in a way that prepares them for the test. This test preparation is great practice for work. Frequently, at work, students will be asked to process large amounts of information in preparation for a presentation or meeting. School provides a great foundation for the development of this skill.

Answer Questions Under Pressure

Taking a test is the most intense and pressure-packed experience that students face at school. Unfortunately, many young people succumb to the pressure and do not do as well as they should on these tests. Other students rise to the occasion and excel at taking tests. At work, employees frequently find themselves in high-pressure situations. The tests that students take in school help them to learn to succeed in these high-pressure situations.

Accept Criticism

For many people, the biggest challenge of work is having their performance reviewed. It is difficult to have their boss tell them what they are doing wrong. Most people do not like having their performance reviewed. They therefore do not handle criticism at work very well. Consequently, they are not successful at work because they were considered bad employees. The tests that students take at school provide a clear indication of how well they are doing. Students learn to accept these test results and study harder if they did not do well. Accepting the criticism provided by tests in school is great preparation for accepting criticism at work.

---

7. Completing an Assignment on Time

Deadlines are an important part of school and work. At school, students are required to complete reading assignments, problem sets, writing assignments, and presentations by a certain day and time. Likewise, employees are asked to complete memos, budgets, and presentations by a certain day and time. School provides excellent training on completing assignments on time. Students who effectively complete their school assignments on time should be able to complete work projects on time.

8. Interacting with Different People

The growing diversity of both schools and places of work makes the ability to effectively interact with people of different backgrounds, cultures, and skills extremely important. At school, the most successful students learn to treat all people with respect. They recognize that "variety is the spice of life" and go out of their way to make friendships with diverse groups of people. Students who are used to developing close relationships with people of different backgrounds will be much better prepared for a diverse work environment. Unfortunately, students who are used to interacting only with people like themselves often have difficulty working with people of different backgrounds. School therefore can potentially teach students how to succeed in a diverse work environment.

9. Teamwork

Schools are recognizing that teaching students about teamwork is an important part of the learning process. There are many more group project assignments than there were 10 years ago. Students who excel in these team projects will be better prepared for work. Organizations recognize that small diverse teams of people typically outperform large groups or groups with little diversity. They are therefore interested in hiring students who have the ability to excel in small diverse teams.

10. Computer Skills

Technology has become the foundation of learning at school. Students must learn how to effectively utilize the computer to excel in their school work. Likewise, technology has revolutionized the world of work. Employees must learn how to use standard business computer software. They must know how to use wordprocessing, financial, database, and presentation software to complete their work assignments. School teaches students how to effectively use technology to complete both school and work assignments.

RECOMMENDATION

Many students do not do well in school because they fail to see the relevance of school work. Hopefully, if you are one of these students, this chapter has inspired you to rededicate yourself to doing well in school. Now that you know the connection between success at school and success in a job, school work should be a lot more fun. No matter how well you have done in school in the past, you should now focus your efforts in school on developing important business skills. It is extremely important for you to assess your personal strengths and weaknesses by completing the BUSINESS SKILLS EVALUATION on the next page.

BUSINESS SKILLS EVALUATION

It is important for you to know your current business strengths and weaknesses. You should therefore evaluate your business skills. Please grade each of your business skills below from 5 to 1 and be as honest as you possibly can. The rating scale is as follows:

5 = Excellent
4 = Very Good
3 = Good
2 = Poor
1 = No Skills in This Area

A. ____ Verbal Communication Skills

B. ____ Reading Comprehension Skills

C. ____ Written Communication Skills

D. ____ Self-Discipline

E. ____ Problem-Solving Skills

F. ____ Test-Taking Skills

G. ____ Completing an Assignment on Time

H. ____ Interacting with Different People

I. ____ Teamwork

J. ____ Computer Skills

By completing this evaluation, you will have a much better idea of the areas that you need to improve. You should therefore work harder at school to improve the business skills that you gave a grade of 3 or less so that you can be more successful at work.

CHAPTER 3

What Kind of Job
Should I Look For?

The Three Sectors

Unfortunately, most students put very little thought into the type of job that they should pursue. They simply search for any job that is near their home or dormitory. Students will spend considerable time researching a paper. However, they usually make no effort to do research on potential job opportunities. As a result, many students end up taking jobs that they dislike. More importantly, these jobs provide no benefits or skills training that could be useful in a future career. One of the main reasons that students do very little job research is that they are intimidated by the world of work. The different sectors, industries, and professions are very confusing. This chapter is focused on taking the mystery out of the world of work.

Most people have heard of job opportunities in corporations, government, or nonprofits. However, many people do not understand that there are three very different sectors. These sectors are the following:

1. Public Sector
2. Private Sector
3. Civic Sector

The public, private, and civic sectors are all extremely different. It is important to understand these three sectors to gain insight into the different job and career opportunities available. Each of these sectors are described below:

1. Public Sector

The public sector includes all federal, state, and local government entities. This includes municipalities, public school districts, county governments, state governments, and the federal government. Public sector organizations provide goods and services that cannot be effectively provided by the private and civic sectors.

2. Private Sector

The private sector includes all organizations that were founded to make a profit. This includes corporations, law firms, and consulting firms. Private sector organizations provide the most career advancement and money-making opportunities for employees.

3. Civic Sector

The civic sector is sometimes called the "Nonprofit Sector." It includes all nonprofit organizations. Most of these entities were founded to help people or communities. This includes social service organizations, education organizations, health care organizations, or associations. Civic sector organizations typically provide opportunities to help people with common interests or people who are less fortunate.

Career Opportunities in the Sectors

Within each sector, there are multiple professional positions. Students that are serious about their career opportunities must take time to find out what career options exist in each sector. We list some of the options in each of the sectors below. Unfortunately, we cannot list every career option available. However, the list below will help students begin their research on career options.

Public Sector Positions

a) Municipal Government – Employee
b) Municipal Government – Elected Official
c) Public School – Employee
d) County Government – Employee
e) County Government – Elected Official
f) Public University – Employee
g) State Government – Employee
h) State Government – Elected Official
i) Federal Government – Employee
j) Federal Government – Elected Official

The public sector career options include opportunities to work as a government employee or work as an elected official. Some of the benefits of working as a government employee include job security, regular hours, and consistent work responsibilities. As an elected official there is great influence, very little job security, long hours, and tremendous public scrutiny. We encourage every student to visit a library or search the Internet for more information about public sector career opportunities.

Private Sector Positions

a) Entrepreneur
b) Business – Executive
c) Business – Operations Employee
d) Business – Administrative Employee
e) Medicine – Doctor
f) Medicine – Nurse
g) Medicine – Administrative Employee
h) Law – Lawyer
i) Law – Administrative Employee
j) Law – Operations Employee
k) Professional Services – Consultant
l) Professional Services – Accountant
m) Professional Services – Operations Employee

The private sector career options include working as an administrative employee doing clerical work in business, medicine, or law. Other career options include selling products, managing technology, or working on general operations in business, medicine, law, and professional services. Finally, the most financially successful employees in the private sector become entrepreneurs, business executives, lawyers, consultants, or accountants who provide technical advice and oversee the operations of the company they work for. We encourage every student to visit a library or search the Internet for more information about private sector career opportunities.

Civic Sector Positions

a) Social Services – Staff
b) Social Services – Volunteer
c) Health Care –Executives
d) Health Care – Volunteer
e) Education – Staff
f) Education – Volunteer
g) Environment – Staff
h) Environment – Volunteer
i) Association – Staff
j) Association – Volunteer

The civic sector career options include serving as staff for nonprofit organizations. Staff typically oversees the daily operations of a nonprofit. These positions are especially rewarding because they play important roles in helping to improve the lives of others. These options also include helping nonprofit organizations by serving as a volunteer. These unpaid positions often provide outstanding work experience that leads to some excellent positions with high pay. Most major hospitals are nonprofit organizations. There are many outstanding career options as medical professionals and operations employees. We encourage every student to visit a library or search the Internet for more information about civic sector career opportunities.

The positions described in this chapter are a small sample of the career options available to students. We encourage students to utilize a five-step process to determine what job they should look for. The five steps are:

1. Determine what sector and career interests you.
2. Conduct research on job opportunities.
3. Meet with people who hold these positions.
4. Find out what jobs provide career training.
5. Interview for those jobs.

1. Determine What Sector and Career Interests You

The very first step in determining what job you should look for is identifying which sector interests you the most. Because the private sector has the most jobs, most students feel compelled to only look for jobs in this sector. However, they may miss out on some high paying jobs that are much more interesting in the public and civic sectors. Once you identify the sector (or sectors) you are most interested in, you should research career opportunities in that sector. Use the Internet to identify as many career opportunities as you can to get an idea of what your long-term options are.

2. Conduct Research on Job Opportunities

Once you have identified the sector and the career opportunities that you are interested in, you should find out what organizations are the best for people who are in the career you are interested in pursuing. The best way to do this is to ask someone who is in this career. If you do not have access to someone in this career, you should search the Internet for relevant company information or ask a counselor in your school for advice on researching job opportunities.

3. Meet with People Who Hold the Positions That Interest You

Doing career and job research on the Internet or at a library is a great start. However, the best information comes from meeting with people who are in the careers you are interested in pursuing. Unfortunately, many students have no idea how to identify these individuals or how to set up a meeting with them. In addition, some students are intimidated by these successful people and are afraid to ask them detailed career questions. Students who do not know people in a targeted profession should first ask family and friends if they know anyone in the profession. If family and friends do not know anyone in the profession, students should speak to their school counselors for help in setting up a meeting with someone in the targeted career. If school counselors cannot help, then students should take the initiative to contact someone in the Human Resources (HR) Division of a company that interests them and ask them if they could meet to discuss careers with the company. Surprisingly, many HR professionals will meet with students who have the initiative to call them about career opportunities. However, many will not meet with students so it is best to keep calling different companies.

4. Find Out What Jobs Provide Career Training

Unfortunately, most jobs offered to students do not provide the training necessary to advance to senior levels in a chosen career. Nevertheless, these jobs can still provide great work experience. These positions are typically designed to be short-term and do not have a track that leads to a specific career. Often, these jobs are designed for students who will work 2-4 years before going to graduate school. Fortunately, there are some jobs that are designed to lead to specific careers. Banks and other financial institutions often have management training programs that provide graduating students with an opportunity to work in different parts of the organization and work their way up to be a senior manager.

5. Interview for Those Jobs

Once you have researched the career and jobs that you are interested in pursuing, you should apply to interview for these positions. Every interview that you participate in should be a learning experience. Interviews will not only help you improve your interview skills, they will help you learn more about the career and job opportunities available in the company.

RECOMMENDATION

You should take the time necessary to do thorough research about job and career opportunities. If you do, you will probably learn a great deal about the world of work and begin to develop a passion for a particular sector, industry, and career. To determine the career that you should pursue, you should know your career preferences. There are far too many jobs and careers to list in one chapter. However, it is a fun exercise to rank the careers that interest you. The table on the next page allows you to do this type of ranking.

RANKING OF CAREER PREFERENCES

The list below is a random list of 20 potential careers. This list does not include all of the great careers and is not intended to be a complete list of potential careers. However, it should inspire you to think seriously about your career interests. Rank (1-20) the careers listed below in order of interest to you (1 being most important). If you are not familiar with some of these careers, you should research them in your school library or on the Internet.

A. ____ School Teacher

B. ____ College Professor

C. ____ Nonprofit Executive Director

D. ____ Doctor

E. ____ School Administrator

F. ____ Lawyer

G. ____ Police Officer

H. ____ Fire Official

I. ____ Government Employee

J. ____ Business Executive

K. ____ Engineer

L. ____ Airline Pilot

M. ____ Accountant

N. ____ Elected Official

O. ____ Entrepreneur

P. ____ Banker

Q. ____ Contractor (Carpenter, Electrician, Landscaper, Painter, Plumber, etc.)

R. ____ Technology Employee

S. ____ Finance Employee

T. ____ Management Consultant

U. ____ Other Career:

_____

_____

By completing this ranking, you will have a better idea of your personal career preferences. Once you have completed this ranking, you should research the jobs that lead to the careers that interest you the most.

CHAPTER 4

What Is a Good Job?

What Is a Good Job

It is not difficult to find a job. However, finding a "good job" is often very difficult for students. Most students do not know what a good job is; they therefore do not know how to find one. Some students think that a job that pays more than minimum wage is a good job. Other students think that a job that allows you to arrive and leave when you want to is a good job. Unfortunately, few students take time to define the characteristics of a good job. They therefore conduct their job search without any idea of what a good job is and end up in a job they don't like. There are many different definitions of a good job. However, the following ten things are common elements of a good job:

1. A good boss
2. Opportunity to learn
3. Stimulating work environment
4. Insight into career opportunities
5. Flexibility
6. Interaction with mentors
7. Access to sponsors
8. Opportunity for promotion
9. Extended employment
10. Pay based on work load

We describe each of the characteristics of a good job on the following pages.

1. A Good Boss

A common saying of human resources executives is that "people quit because of their boss, not because of their company." People usually leave their job because they have a bad boss, not because they are working for a bad company. Most employees' view of their company is based on who gives them direction. Unfortunately, many bosses are patronizing, controlling, rude, and lack leadership skills. People who work for these bosses usually do not have a favorable view of their employer. Good bosses are typically flexible, understanding, polite, and supportive. They provide clear direction and guidance, and take pride in enhancing the skills and abilities of the people reporting to them. People who work for these bosses have a very positive view of their employer. Students interviewing for a job should find out as much as they can about the person they will be reporting to at work. The quality of their boss can make the difference between having a good job and having a horrible job.

2. Opportunity To Learn

Students should be focused on finding jobs that provide learning opportunities. A good job will teach students about jobs they had never been exposed to previously. It will help them learn skills that will enhance their success in a future career. A good job will also expose students to outstanding leaders who will be able to teach students how to excel in the world of work.

3. Stimulating Work Environment

One common myth about the world of work is that the best jobs are the easiest. However, the total opposite is true. Jobs that are easy are often incredibly boring. When you do not have much to do, the day drags on and goes by very slowly. However, when you have a job with a lot to do, the day is over before you know it because you are constantly being stimulated intellectually. A good job has a work environment where you have a lot of work that stimulates you by challenging you to do more than you ever thought was possible.

4. Insight into Career Opportunities

All too often students take jobs without thinking about their future career. It is extremely important for students to take jobs that will give them some insight into potential career opportunities. If they are interested in potentially being a business executive, they should find a job in the business of their choice. If they have an interest in medicine, they should find a job in a hospital. A good job will help students learn more about the career opportunities they are considering.

5. Flexibility

A good job provides for some flexibility in hours and responsibility. Typically, this flexibility is only earned by outstanding employees. A boss is more likely to allow a hard-working employee to have flexible work hours than an average employee. Likewise, employees who do excellent work are more likely to have flexibility in their job responsibilities. Students can only earn job flexibility if they work significantly harder than other employees.

6. Interaction with Mentors

A mentor is someone who provides solid advice on ways to excel at work and in life. A good job encourages interaction with mentors. Students should look for jobs that place a strong emphasis on finding mentors for employees. An effective mentor can help students succeed in their current job and find the career that is best suited to their interests and skills.

7. Access to Sponsors

Many people confuse mentors and sponsors. Mentors provide career and life advice. However, they do not have a direct impact on the career of their mentees. Sponsors, on the other hand, have a direct impact on the career of the people they are sponsoring. A sponsor has control over an employee's career. They have input into the salary that employees are paid.

They also determine if an employee will receive a promotion. The sponsor of most employees is their boss. They therefore should do what they can to exceed their boss's expectations so that he or she will actively sponsor them. Students should search for jobs that provide great opportunities for them to work closely with their boss and earn their sponsorship.

8. Opportunities for Promotion

Most students interview for a job without thinking about promotion opportunities. Employers want to hire students who are interested in getting promoted. They are less interested in students who are not thinking beyond the job they are seeking. Workers interested in getting promoted will work harder and become better employees. Students who do not think about getting promoted typically do not take their job very seriously. They are therefore poor employees. A good job will provide plenty of opportunities for promotion.

9. Extended Employment

A good job will provide plenty of opportunity for continued employment beyond the initial hiring (if the employee is outstanding). Students, who are fortunate to have a job that they enjoy and excel at, will want to continue their work beyond the initial hiring period. Summer interns may want to continue to make money well into the school year. Part-time employees may want to become full-time employees. Full-time employees may want a position with more responsibility.

10. Pay Based on Work Load

A job paying minimum wage may be sufficient for most students. Unfortunately, many of these jobs do not pay much more for positions of greater intensity and responsibility. A good job will include opportunities for promotion and increased pay based on the work load and level of responsibility of the worker.

RECOMMENDATION

Now that you have an idea of the elements of a good job, you should begin developing a list of positions that have one or more of these elements. Learn as much as you can about good job opportunities from friends, family, and the Internet. You should also determine the elements of a good job that interest you the most. The best way to do this is to complete the ranking list on the next page. You should find that this exercise will force you to reflect on the elements of a job that will determine whether it is a great job or just a good job. It will also motivate you to think in depth about who you are and what is important to you.

RANKING OF ELEMENTS OF A GOOD JOB

You may not agree with the priority ranking of the ten elements of a good job in this chapter. It is very important for you to understand which elements are most important to you. Consequently, you should rank the ten elements of a good job (1 being most important) below:

A.   _____ A Good Boss

B.   _____ Opportunity To Learn

C.   _____ Stimulating Work Environment

D.   _____ Insight into Career Opportunities

E.   _____ Flexibility

F.   _____ Interaction with Mentors

G.   _____ Access to Sponsors

H.   _____ Opportunity for Promotion

I.   _____ Extended Employment

J.   _____ Pay Based on Work Load

K.   _____ Other
          (List Another Element Here: _____)

By completing this ranking, you will be able to target your job search to those jobs that have the elements that are most important to you. This exercise should be very informative and a lot of fun.

CHAPTER 5

What Do Employers Look For?

Ten Things Employers Look For

Students must have a thorough understanding of what employers look for in potential employees before they can get a good job. Every employer has different needs. However, all employers look for the following ten things in their employees:

1. Positive presence
2. Strong verbal communication skills
3. Understanding of the organization's objectives
4. Project management skills
5. Past success
6. People skills
7. Problem-solving skills
8. Strong work ethic
9. Project-planning skills
10. Career goals

These traits represent the skills that make some people great employees. Students interested in succeeding in a job and career should attempt to develop these skills long before they prepare for their first interview.

1. Positive Presence

There has been a lot written about the power of dressing for success. Likewise, there has been a great deal written about the importance of having strong verbal communication skills at work. However, little has been written about the importance of presence. A person's work presence is a combination of what they wear, how they stand, how well they interact with people, how confident they are, and how well they listen. Employers are looking to hire people that wear appropriate business clothes, communicate well, exude confidence (not arrogance) in their abilities, stand up straight, work well with different people, and listen well. Students should attempt to develop each of these traits in order to establish a positive presence (well before their first job interview).

2. Strong Verbal Communication Skills

Verbal communication skills are discussed in many of the chapters of this book because they are the single most important trait in business. Most communication between employees occurs through face-to-face discussions. Employers therefore look for employees who are exceptional communicators. Students who want to excel at work must do everything they can to enhance their ability to convey their thoughts in words.

3. Understanding of the Organization's Objectives

Employers want to hire people who have a passion for the company they work for. They want employees to know about the organization's mission, objectives, and business strategy. The Internet allows employees and potential employees to do an incredible amount of research on the company they work for. There is absolutely no excuse for employees not to learn as much as they can about their company from co-workers, company literature, and Internet research. Employers also like employees to understand financial information related to a company's stock price (if it is publicly traded) and/or the organization's budget.

4. Project Management Skills

Contrary to popular opinion every employee is a project manager. They are asked to manage projects of different sizes and durations. The project could be as basic as completing a simple assignment on time or transporting something from one place to another. The project could be extremely complicated and require working with many different people. Employers are therefore looking for people who can complete their assignments on time. They are also looking for employees who have the potential to effectively manage more complicated projects.

5. Past Success

Most employers believe that past success is the best predictor of future success. They are interested in hiring people who have demonstrated past success at school or work. This past success could be outstanding grades or evidence of the successful completion of complicated work assignments. Long before students decide to interview for a job, they should work on demonstrating success in any way that they can in everything that they do.

6. People Skills

The best employees have the ability to work effectively with other people. They work well on team projects, follow directions well, and can inspire their fellow employees to become better co-workers. Employers look for employees with strong people skills because they play an important role in helping organizations increase their productivity and effectiveness.

7. Problem-Solving Skills

Most employees have to make many decisions related to work problems. Frequently, these decisions mean the difference between success and failure. The most effective employees have very good problem-solving skills. They therefore come up with creative solutions to work related problems. Employers desperately look for employees with good problem-solving skills because employees with these skills typically play a critical role in helping an organization succeed.

8. Strong Work Ethic

Employers look for employees who are willing to work as hard as necessary to excel in their positions. The best employees have a strong work ethic. They take their job very seriously and inspire other employees to work hard as well. Employers look for students who have demonstrated that they have a strong work ethic.

9. Planning Skills

Planning is a very important part of a successful organization. All activities of an organization should be planned to ensure that they maximize the organization's effectiveness. The most valuable employees are those that can effectively develop project plans and successfully complete them on time. Employers are looking for employees who have experience in developing and executing project plans. Students can develop these planning skills by taking the lead in planning projects at school.

10. Career Goals

The best employees take their careers very seriously. They focus on doing an exceptional job at work because it will help to further their career. Employees therefore look for employees that have well thought-out career plans. Consequently, students should spend considerable time thinking about their career aspirations.

RECOMMENDATION

Once you have a thorough understanding of the ten traits that most employers look for in future employees, you should evaluate yourself on each of these traits by completing the evaluation on the next page.

EVALUATION OF THE TEN THINGS EMPLOYERS LOOK FOR

It is important for you to reflect on your relative strengths and weaknesses in the ten things employers look for in their employees. The best way to do this is to use the grading system below. Please grade yourself in each of the ten things employers look for in employees from 5 to 1 and be as honest as you possibly can.

5 = Excellent
4 = Very Good
3 = Good
2 = Poor
1 = No Skills in This Area

A. _____ Presence

B. _____ Verbal Communication Skills

C. _____ Understanding of the Organization's Objectives

D. _____ Project Management Skills

E. _____ Past Successes

F. _____ People Skills

G. _____ Problem-Solving Skills

H. _____ Strong Work Ethic

I. _____ Project-Planning Skills

J. _____ Career Goals

By completing this weighting, you will have a much better idea of the areas that you need to improve. You should take the time necessary to address any of the weaknesses that you have in the areas that are important to employers. If you are able to honestly rank yourself either 4 or 5 in each of these areas, you will increase your ability to find the job of your dreams. If possible, start this self-improvement process today by focusing on the development of each of these traits. Typically, the sooner you start this self-development, the more successful you will be at work.

CHAPTER 6

How Do I Create a Resume and Cover Letter?

Applying for a Job

Employers expect applicants for a job to have a document that accurately describes their background and provides insight into their ability to do the job. That document is called a "resume."

A resume is a concise summary of your experiences and skills as they relate to the position you are applying for. It summarizes your accomplishments to demonstrate to an employer why you should be hired. It is not a biography of your life. A resume provides details of your academic, extracurricular, leadership, volunteer, and work experiences. Your resume should be designed to fit the positions you are applying for.

The primary purpose of a resume is to get you an interview and frame your talking points during the interview. A resume is sent to a potential employer with a cover letter describing why you are interested and qualified for the position you are applying for.

There are five key steps in preparing to apply for a job. These are:

1. Identify the position.
2. Describe your background.
3. Understand the resume elements.
4. Complete the resume.
5. Write a cover letter.

---

1. Identify the Position

The first step in preparing to apply for a job is to identify the position(s) you are applying for. As discussed in previous chapters, it is extremely important for you to do extensive research on careers so that you will be able to pursue jobs that will help you achieve your long-term career goals. If you take time to do this research, you will know what jobs you should pursue. This research will help you identify the positions in your area that you should apply for. Once you identify these positions, you should (if possible) get a copy of the job description. This description will list the responsibilities of the job, the skills required to succeed in this job, and the type of experience that is required (or preferred) for the job. This information will be extremely helpful as you begin to develop a resume and cover letter.

---

2. Describe Your Background

The second step in preparing to apply for a job is to make a list of your activities over the last 3 to 5 years. Students should list paid work, volunteer positions, internships, extracurricular activities, awards, and anything else in their life that they consider unique. This initial list does not have to be in any specific format. However, ideally the list should name the activity and describe in one paragraph what the activity entailed, why it is important, and how it demonstrates that you will succeed in the position you are applying for.

For example, if a student wants to pursue a career as a bank executive and is applying for a position as an intern in a local bank, he could describe his *Intellectual Abilities, Paid Work Experience, Volunteer Work Experience, Extracurricular Leadership Experience,* and *Miscellaneous Achievements* as follows:

Intellectual Abilities — *High School Academic Experience*

When I started high school, I was not a very good student because I did not take my homework seriously. However, in my Junior year, I discovered how important doing well in school is to getting a good job. I therefore applied myself at school for the first time and received all A's and B's. I am interested in banking because I discovered I have a passion and talent for math.

Paid Work Experience — *Cashier at McDonalds*

For the last two years, I have been one of the most successful cashiers at the local McDonalds Restaurant. I excelled at customer service. I took my job very seriously and always arrived on time. I was very responsive to my manager and worked very well with my co-workers. I was always willing to work overtime as needed. Most importantly, I became extremely skilled at managing the thousands of dollars I received a day from customers. This experience of managing money and working with others will help me be a successful bank employee.

Volunteer Work Experience — *Soup Kitchen Volunteer*

In the last year, I volunteered my time to serve food to the homeless at the local soup kitchen. I played a leadership role in helping to prepare the meal, set up the tables, serve the food, and clean up after the meal. This position not only helped me understand the value of helping the less fortunate, it accelerated the development of my leadership skills which will serve me well as a bank employee.

Extracurricular Leadership Experience — *Captain of the Tennis Team*

I did not know how to play tennis when I started high school. However, after taking free lessons through the local United States Tennis Association (USTA) National Junior Tennis League (NJTL) chapter, practicing a lot and watching the US Open every year on television, I learned to play tennis. I became good enough to play number 1 on my high school tennis team and serve as Captain of the team as a senior. Under my leadership, the team became more cohesive and worked harder than ever to improve our record. This drive to be successful combined with my leadership experience will help me be a successful bank employee.

Miscellaneous Achievements — *Fluent in Spanish, Photo Contest Winner*

I enjoy learning new languages. I did well in Spanish in school so I decided to become fluent in the language. I am now fluent in Spanish. In addition, I enjoy photography and had the great honor of winning the Annual Any Town Photography contest.

These examples demonstrate how to list your academic, work, and extracurricular experience in a way that relates this experience to the job you are applying for. You may not have the type of experience listed in the example. However, it is very easy for you to quickly get some volunteer and extracurricular experience that will look good on your resume.

---

3. Understand the Resume Elements

The third step in preparing to apply for a job is to understand the elements of an effective resume. The resume should have the applicant's name, home address, phone number, and email address on the top. However, the other elements of the resume make the difference between a good resume and an outstanding resume. It is therefore extremely important to understand the relevance of each section of the resume. The key sections are the:

a) Education Section
b) Academic Statement Section
c) Work Experience Section
d) Extracurricular Experience Section
e) Achievements Section
f) Reference Statement

Education Section

The *Education Section* follows the personal information at the top of the resume. The purpose of this section is to highlight your academic success. In this section, you should list the high school and (if applicable) college you are attending or graduated from. Employers want to know that you have taken your school work seriously. They believe that success in school translates to success at work. If you have done well in school, you should list your grade point average and any academic honors that you have received. If your overall grade point average (GPA) is a B (3.0) or below, you should probably not list it on your resume. However, if you did not do well in your freshman and sophomore years but have done well in your junior and senior years, you may want to list your junior and senior GPA (see the sample resume).

Academic Statement Section

Students that do not have a high GPA may want to include an *Academic Statement* like the one included in the sample resume (based on the *Intellectual Abilities* information that was included in the original list of experience). Sometimes students have a very good reason why they have not done well in school. One of the most impressive reasons for this is that they had to work 15 or more hours a week to help to support their family. It is important for employers to know that students who may not have high GPAs are hard workers. A well-written *Academic Statement* can convince employers to hire students because of their work ethic.

Work Experience Section

The *Work Experience Section* follows the *Academic Statement Section* (if you have one). In many ways, it is the most important section of the resume. It tells potential employers what jobs you have had and how well you have done in those jobs. You should therefore put a lot of thought and effort into writing this section.

You should begin by listing each of the companies that you have worked for and the positions you have held. Your volunteer work should be listed in the same way you list your paid jobs. Most students do not realize how valuable volunteer experience can be on a resume. Frequently, student volunteers are given more responsibility than their counterparts in paid positions. They therefore have more impressive things to write about their work experience. You should describe the business-related capabilities that you developed in paid and volunteer positions.

The key business traits that employers are looking for include people management, communication, computer, financial and organizational skills. They are also looking for employees who are good problem solvers and hard workers. If possible, describe how your position helped you develop one or more of these business skills.

Extracurricular Experience Section

The *Extracurricular Experience Section* follows the *Work Experience Section*. In this section, you should highlight your most impressive activities out of the classroom and away from your paid or volunteer work. Employers like to hire students who have been leaders in clubs, sports teams, musical groups, etc. They believe that if you were accepted by your classmates as a leader, then you have the ability to work well with others. You should therefore make every effort to assume a leadership role in any organization that you are a part of at school or in the community.

Achievements Section

In the *Achievements Section* of your resume, you should list any impressive accomplishments that have not been listed in the other sections. You may have received an award from a community organization, speak another language, or have special computer programming skills. It is extremely important for you to list this information. This information often impresses interviewers enough to convince them to offer you a job.

Reference Statement

It is extremely important to have people verify that your resume is accurate and you have accomplished what you say you accomplished. You should therefore identify three people who will be willing to tell potential employers that you will be an outstanding worker. These individuals are called "references." Your resume should end with the statement "References are available upon request." In other words, you should have a sheet that lists the name, phone number, email address, company, and job title of the three (or more) people who are willing to be your references. You should bring several copies of this sheet to your interviews and give them to the potential employer if asked.

4. Complete the Resume

Now that you have identified the position that you want, listed your experience and accomplishments, and developed a good understanding of the resume sections, you should write your resume. At first, writing your resume may seem to be very difficult. The key is to get some sample resumes from friends, family, or the Internet and start writing. Please note that the format of their resume may be slightly different because they are older and have much more work experience. One big difference is the placement of your education. Once you have a great deal of work experience, you will list your education at the end of the resume. Another difference may be the length of the resume. Your entire resume should be on one page. However, people who have worked for many years could have a resume of two pages or more.

It will probably take four or five drafts before you develop a resume that you like. The experience of developing your resume at first seems like it is very difficult. However, the more you practice, the better you get at developing a resume. This skill is extremely important because you will be developing new resumes for most of your life. Every time you get a new job, are involved in a significant activity, or win a special award, you should immediately add it to your resume. Unfortunately, most people do not understand how important it is to manage their resume. This document can help to determine how much you make, what your major at school should be, where you live, and what leadership positions you hold.

Frequently, resumes demonstrate that someone has good skills and experience in one area. However, it may also highlight weakness in other areas. For example, some people may have majored in marketing in college and worked for several prestigious marketing companies. Their resume is very strong in marketing. However, it may be weak in finance. Employers will want to see this person get finance experience through work or college to balance out their skills and experience. They should make a special effort to get this experience to enhance their resume and employment opportunities. It is therefore extremely important to think about taking jobs or volunteering your time in a way that enhances your resume.

On the next page, we provide a sample resume for Jane Johnson using the information we wrote when we described her background. This should be a helpful guide as you develop your resume.

Jane Johnson

100 Main Street, Any Town, Any State, 11111
(444) 222-0000 Johnson123@email.com

June 10, XXXX

Education

Washington High School – Any Town, Any State
Junior and Senior Year GPA: 3.25
Math Honors
English Honors

Academic Statement

When I started high school, I was not a very good student because I did not take my homework seriously. However, in my junior year, I discovered how important doing well in school is to getting a good job. I therefore applied myself at school for the first time and received all A's and B's. I was able to do this while working 10 hours a week to help to support my family. I am interested in banking because I discovered I have a talent for math and a passion for investing money.

Work Experience

McDonalds, Inc.   Any Town, Any State
Cashier   2006 – Present

I was hired to take orders and serve food for customers of the restaurant. I excelled at customer service and became one of the senior cashiers in the store. Because of my outstanding performance, I have the honor of always being the first employee asked to work overtime. I developed an exceptional ability to work with different managers and co-workers and had the best on-time record of any employee at any level. This incredible experience helped me to develop the skills necessary to succeed in a corporate environment. I successfully handled money transactions with customers and excelled in all of the money collection and tracking responsibilities of the job. The financial aspects of the position inspired me to pursue a career in banking.

Any Town Soup Kitchen   Any Town, Any State
Volunteer   2007 – Present

I collected food from local residents for the homeless and assisted in the preparation of food at Any Town Soup Kitchen. I also served food to hungry residents and managed the set-up before the meal and clean-up

(continued)

after the meal. I discovered that I had a talent for interacting with other people and developed excellent relationships with both the staff and customers. This experience served as great training for future paid positions.

Extracurricular Experience

High School Tennis Team
Captain

I did not know how to play tennis when I started high school. However, I took community tennis lessons and taught myself through hours and hours of practice in addition to watching the US Open every year on television. I became good enough to play number 1 on my high school tennis team and serve as Captain of the team as a senior. Under my leadership, the team became more cohesive and worked harder than ever to improve our games. This drive to be successful and leadership experience will help me be a successful employee.

Achievements

- Fluent in Spanish
- Winner of the Any Town 2007 Still Life Photography Contest

References will be provided upon request.

---

5. *Write a Cover Letter*

The letter that you send to employers with your resume is called a "cover letter." Your cover letter and resume should complement each another. They work together to present you as a qualified candidate for the job that you are pursuing. The cover letter should be custom designed for each potential job and highlight relevant aspects of the resume that will appeal to the potential employer. Resumes show the potential employer that you have the skills and experience necessary to successfully do the work that the job requires.

Cover letters demonstrate that you are familiar with the organization and have a passionate interest in joining the company. Good cover letters reflect the personality, communication skills, intellect, and enthusiasm of the applicant. In addition, they show great attention to detail. Many people are passed over for interviews because of mistakes in their cover letters or resumes. Employers believe that if you are not willing to take the time to ensure that your cover letter and resume are perfect, you will not be willing to take the time necessary to carefully do your work. You should therefore have multiple people proofread your cover letters and resume.

A cover letter should be addressed to the specific individual and company who will process your application. Remember, the resume is a generic advertisement of your skills and experience. The cover letter allows you to tailor your application to each position you are interviewing for. The letter should identify the position for which you are applying. The letter should demonstrate your passionate interest in the position and knowledge about the work of the company. It should also highlight your qualifications for the position. The three questions the cover letter should answer are:

a) **Why do you want to work at this specific company?**
b) **How does your background qualify you for the specific position?**
c) **Why should you be granted an interview for the position?**

The cover letter should be in paragraph form. The very first paragraph should be three or four sentences explaining what job you are applying for, how you learned about the job, and what your qualifications are for the job.

There are two basic types of cover letters. The first is the type used to respond to an advertisement or a request for your resume. You are writing this cover letter to an employer who is looking to hire someone for a specific position and is expecting to receive requests for an interview. *Sample Cover Letter 1* is this type of letter. The second type of cover letter is one written to someone who is not actively looking to hire someone for a specific position. This letter is written to convince a company to interview you for a position that they have not publicly advertised. *Sample Cover Letter 2* is this type of letter.

Jane Johnson

100 Main Street, Any Town, Any State, 11111
(444) 222-0000 Johnson123@email.com

March 20, XXXX

Mr. Harry Hire
Human Resources Director
ABC Bank
1000 Any Street
Any Town, Any State 22222

Dear Mr. Hire,

Your advertisement for the position of Bank Teller in the March 19 edition of the Tribune caught my attention. I was drawn to the advertisement by my strong interest in using my math skills in a part-time/summer position. I am very impressed by the information that I found on the Internet about your organization. This information convinced me that ABC Bank is the perfect place for me to work.

As you can see from my resume, I have significantly more work and leadership experience than most people my age. This experience combined with my work ethic and math skills will enable me to add value to your organization. In addition, I have an interest in a career in banking. My long-term goal is to become a senior executive in banking after I finish my education.

I would like to meet with you to discuss any open positions at the bank. If you would like to arrange an interview, please call me at (444) 222-0000 or email me at Johnson123@email.com .

Sincerely,

Jane Johnson

Jane Johnson

100 Main Street, Any Town, Any State, 11111
(444) 222-0000 Johnson123@email.com

March 20, XXXX

Mr. Steven Supervisor
Bank Manager
XYZ Bank
3000 Any Street
Any Town, Any State 33333

Dear Mr. Supervisor,

As a successful student with a passion for money management, I am writing to request information about part-time and summer employment opportunities at XYZ Bank. I am interested in a position that will enable me to demonstrate my exceptional work ethic and strong math skills. I am very impressed by the information that I found on the Internet about your organization. This information convinced me that XYZ Bank is the perfect place for me to work.

As you can see from my attached resume, I have more work and leadership experience than most students my age. This experience combined with my interest in banking will enable me at add value to your organization immediately. My long-term goal is to become a senior executive in banking after I finish my education. A position with XYZ Bank is an important first step in helping me achieve this goal.

I would like to meet with you to discuss any open positions at the bank. If you would like to arrange an interview, please call me at (444) 222-0000 or email me at Johnson123@email.com .

Sincerely,

Jane Johnson

RECOMMENDATION

You should begin the preparation necessary to apply for a job as soon as possible. Identifying good job opportunities, developing a quality resume, and writing a strong cover letter takes time. The sooner you begin this important work, the better. You will be surprised how effective well constructed resumes and cover letters will be in your job search. One of the best ways to measure your progress against the goal of developing an effective resume and cover letter is to complete the RESUME AND COVER LETTER CHECKLIST on the next page.

RESUME AND COVER LETTER CHECKLIST

The list below contains each of the activities you should complete to develop an effective resume and cover letter. Please check each of the items that you have completed below:

1. _____ I have thoroughly researched job opportunities.

2. _____ I have identified the position(s) I would like to interview for.

3. _____ I have completed a list of my activities over the last 5 years.

4. _____ I have completed the *Education Section* of my resume.

5. _____ I have completed the *Academic Statement Section* of my resume (if applicable).

6. _____ I have completed the *Work Experience Section* of my resume.

7. _____ I have completed the *Extracurricular Experience Section* of my resume.

8. _____ I have completed the *Achievements Section* of my resume.

9. _____ I have identified references and completed the *"References will be provided by request" Section*.

10. _____ I have completed the necessary cover letters.

Once you have completed each of the ten things on the RESUME AND COVER LETTER CHECKLIST, you are ready to send these documents to potential employers. Do not send resumes or cover letters to potential employers until you have completed each activity on the checklist.

CHAPTER 7

What are Good Interview Skills?

Interviewing Overview

Now that you have completed your resume and cover letter you should learn how to interview. Unfortunately, most students take interviewing for granted. They treat it as an informal discussion instead of the most important part of the hiring process. If students are serious about finding a job they should know the following three things:

1. How to prepare for an interview.
2. What most employers are looking for.
3. What the most common interview questions are.

---

1. How To Prepare for an Interview

All too often students do not prepare for job interviews. They therefore do a poor job of responding to questions from potential employers and frequently have difficulty finding employment. There are five key things that you must do to prepare for an interview. These are:

a) Prepare yourself.
b) Know the company.
c) Know the job.
d) Prepare questions.
e) Do practice interviews.

Prepare Yourself

The first step in preparing for an interview is preparing yourself to be interviewed. This may seem to be very obvious. However, many people do not take the time necessary to effectively prepare themselves for an interview. They do not understand interview etiquette or what type of questions to expect. They do not know how to respond to questions or what questions to ask. In addition, they do not know what to wear to an interview. The five things you must do to effectively prepare yourself for an interview are:

1) Know your resume.
2) Dress for success.
3) Plan to be on time.
4) Enhance your communication skills.
5) Understand interview etiquette.

1) Know Your Resume

You should begin preparing yourself for the interview by reviewing your resume and cover letter. The interviewer will ask you questions based on the information in these two documents. It is essential that you memorize everything that is on your resume and be able to speak eloquently about your skills and experience. One of the most common mistakes that many people make is not being able to answer questions about their resume in the interview. This tells the employer that the person has either lied on their resume or that they are not taking the job opportunity very seriously.

2) Dress for Success

The second you walk into the company or the interview waiting area, you will be judged based on how you present yourself. If you are wearing dirty wrinkled clothes, it tells potential employers that you are a sloppy person who does not have the confidence necessary to succeed in the job. In advance of the interview, you should find out what type of clothes are acceptable for the interview. You may have to wear traditional business clothes (suits or dresses). If this is the case, make sure that you have at least one formal interview outfit in your closet. If the interview attire is more casual, make sure that you have clean wrinkle-free, fairly conservative outfits to wear.

3) Plan To Be On Time

You should never be late for an interview. The first rule of interviewing is always be early. Allow more time than you need to get to the interview location. Sometimes you will have to fill out some forms before the interview, so give yourself plenty of extra time. It is a good idea to arrive 15 minutes or more before the interview. There is no good excuse for being late. Be honest with yourself about your past tendencies. Some people are always late. Others are always early. If you are a habitually late person, you should allow yourself a lot of extra time to get to the interview. If you are late for your interview, it tells the interviewer that you are not very interested in the job.

4) Enhance Your Communication Skills

Your communication skills are a key factor in how you are evaluated by the potential employer. No matter what job you are interviewing for, you will have to do a great deal of communicating with supervisors and fellow employees. Most problems in an organization are caused by poor communication. Employers are therefore looking for people who are good communicators. They want to hire employees who have a positive attitude, enjoy being around people, are good listeners, and can effectively convey a message in the work environment. The slang language that you may use with your friends is typically unacceptable in the work place. You should attempt to speak in the same manner as your interviewer. If this is difficult for you, it is essential that you change the way you speak. You should practice speaking in a way that will be appropriate for the position you are seeking.

5) *Understand Interview Etiquette*

You will typically be sitting in a waiting room with other potential candidates before you are interviewed. It is important to be extremely polite and courteous with everyone you meet. All too often, students go to a job interview with the idea that they only have to be polite to their interviewer. You should be extremely friendly with the person who signs you in for the interview. In addition, you should be courteous with other individuals in the waiting room. Employers will take note of everything that you do before, during, and after the interview.

If you have a great interview but are rude to the receptionist or other interviewees, you will not get a job offer. It is said that many interviews are decided in the first 30 seconds. When you walk into the room to greet the interviewer, always give him or her a very firm handshake, look them directly in the eyes, and say "nice to meet you." This will tell the employer that you have the self-confidence and manners necessary to succeed in the work environment. All too often students have a weak handshake and look away when they meet the interviewer. This tells the potential employer that students he or she is interviewing may not really believe that they can succeed in the job.

Some job candidates do not know how to be polite during the interview. They may interrupt the interviewer, ignore what they are saying, cough without covering their mouth, or behave in some other manner that is inappropriate. It is essential that all job candidates understand basic interviewing etiquette before an interview.

Know the Company

There is absolutely no excuse for not knowing a lot about an organization before you interview. Every organization has a website with important information about what they do and who their clients are. You should study that website and memorize key information that will impress the interviewer. If there is not enough information on the website, you should ask someone in the company, nonprofit, or government agency about the organization. If you do not know anyone who works for the organization, you should find someone who works for a similar type of organization and ask him or her about the organization interviewing you. It is extremely important for you to be proactive about getting this information. Some of the things you should know about the organization include:

1) History
2) Size
3) Mission/Objectives
4) Clients
5) Financial information
6) Main locations
7) Career paths offered
8) Reputation

Know the Job

Once you have learned about the organization, you should attempt to find out everything that you can about the job you are interviewing for. The five key things that you should find out are:

1) What does the job entail?
2) What is the hardest thing about the job?
3) Does the supervisor have a good reputation in the company?
4) Is the company a good place to work?
5) Are there opportunities for promotion?

If you do not know anyone in the organization, you should ask family members or friends if they know anyone in the organization. If they do, you should ask them to ask their contact if you could speak with them for 5 minutes about the job. If no one you know has contacts in the organization, you can call the organization directly and ask to speak to someone in the department where the job is located. They will connect you with someone and you should simply say "I am interviewing for a position with your organization and have five quick questions about the job. Do you have 5 minutes to talk?" More than likely, they will say yes and give you some important inside information that will be helpful for your interview. If word gets back to your interviewer that you called the organization, they will usually be very impressed by your interest in the job. Employers are looking to hire people who have initiative and require little direction. You would be amazed how helpful and honest people will be in organizations.

Prepare Questions

At some point in the interview, you will be asked if you have any questions. All too often, students do not understand that this is their opportunity to shine. They therefore say they do not have any questions. However, good interviewees know that the right questions can indicate interest in a position and knowledge about the company that will impress interviewers. You should therefore prepare insightful questions to ask the interviewer. Some of the questions that you may want to potentially ask include:

1) Have I answered all of your questions?
2) Tell me how you have succeeded in the organization?
3) What skills do you believe are most important for success in the job?
4) What has made the organization successful?
5) How soon do you expect to make a hiring decision?

These questions will indicate that you have a strong interest both in the job and succeeding in the company. If the interview goes longer than anticipated, you may not have time to ask more than one of these questions.

Do Practice Interviews

Probably the most important thing that you can do before an interview is practice. Find a friend, teacher, or parent who is willing to pretend to interview you. The old saying "Practice makes perfect" is absolutely true. By practicing your interviews, you will develop better responses to questions and gain a confidence in your interview skills that will force employers to take your candidacy more seriously. You will learn how to begin interviews better. You will be able to effectively respond to difficult questions and impress the interviewer with your questions. There is no excuse for not practicing your interviews.

2. What Most Employers Are Looking For

It is impossible to know exactly what each interviewer is looking for in an interview. Every interviewer brings personal experiences and biases to the interview. Frequently, in their subconscious, they are looking for people like themselves. They therefore may give hiring preference to people who have similar backgrounds to their own (attended the same school, have a similar work background, or share a hobby). However, good interviewers will evaluate candidates based solely on their interview skills and qualifications for the job. There are ten things most employers are looking for in job candidates in the interview. Employers interview candidates to see if they:

1) Wear appropriate business clothes to the interview.
2) Have strong verbal communication skills.
3) Demonstrate a healthy sense of humor.
4) Can eloquently explain their resume.
5) Have a passion for the company and position.
6) Demonstrate a positive outlook on life.
7) Have a history of managing their time well.
8) Take direction well.
9) Show a strong history of success.
10) Ask insightful questions.

3. What the Most Common Interview Questions Are

It is hard to predict exactly what questions you will be asked in an interview. However, there is some standard information that interviewers need to effectively evaluate candidates. Over the years, human resource executives have developed many different ways to ask questions. However, there are two types of interviews. The first type of interview is called a "Traditional Interview." Most people are familiar with this type of interview where the employer will ask general open-ended questions about a candidate's background and experience.

The second type of interview is called a "Behavioral Interview." In these interviews, employers ask candidates about past examples of behavior in an effort to predict future behavior. They therefore will ask a general question about an experience and then probe for great detail about a specific experience. Different organizations use different interviewing techniques. It is therefore important for you to be prepared for both of these types of interviews. We have therefore listed ten Traditional Interview questions and ten Behavioral Interview Questions. Interviewers may not ask the questions listed below exactly as they are written. However, they will likely ask similar questions to find out the same information.

Ten of the most common Traditional Interview questions are:

1) How did you hear about this position?
2) Why are you interested in this position?
3) What can you tell me about yourself (in two minutes or less)?
4) What have been your most satisfying and disappointing school or work experiences?
5) What supervisory or leadership roles have you held?
6) What can you tell me about your scholastic record?
7) What are your strengths and weaknesses?
8) Why should we hire you?
9) Where do you see yourself in 5 years and 10 years?
10) Do you have any questions for me?

Behavioral Interview questions typically begin with "Tell me about a time when you …" After that initial question, the interviewer will ask a series of follow-up questions to determine what really happened during "that time." Their goal is to find out what work-related skills you demonstrated during that situation. The key to answering this question is to pick a "time" when you handled a difficult situation very well. Ten of the most common Behavioral Interview questions are *Tell me about a time when you …*

1) … were creative in solving a problem.
2) … overcame great obstacles to achieve success.
3) … demonstrated strong leadership.
4) … handled a difficult situation with someone.
5) … worked effectively under pressure.
6) … delegated a project effectively.

7) ...persuaded others to do things your way.

8) ...were unable to complete a project on time.

9) ...made a bad decision.

10)...prioritized the elements of a difficult project.

Interview Follow-up

It is extremely important to remember that just before your interview is finished, you should find out what the next steps are in the interview process and when you will hear the results of the interview. This will show your interest and help you manage your expectations. You should also ask for a business card from your interviewer or at a minimum get his or her mailing address. Once the interview is complete, you should send a thank-you note to your interviewer immediately. If you do not hear the results of your interview a week after the date given by the interviewer, you should call them to check on your status.

RECOMMENDATION

It is essential that you take sufficient time to prepare for a job interview. If you want a particular job, you must learn specifically what employers are looking for in candidates. You must be prepared for the major potential interview questions. Most importantly, you must prepare yourself to do the best job possible in the interview. One way to ensure that you are prepared for an interview is to complete the INTERVIEW PREPARATION CHECKLIST on the next page.

INTERVIEW PREPARATION CHECKLIST

The list below contains each of the activities you should feel, understand, complete, or do to do well in an interview. Please check each of the items that apply below:

1. _____ I feel prepared mentally for the stress of a job interview.

2. _____ I have done extensive research on the company that is interviewing me.

3. _____ I understand the responsibilities of the job I am interviewing for.

4. _____ I have prepared substantive questions for the interviewer.

5. _____ I have practiced my interview technique and understand interview etiquette.

6. _____ I am wearing appropriate clothes for the interview.

7. _____ I have developed strong communications skills that will impress my interviewer.

8. _____ I have thought of ways to inject humor into the interview.

9. _____ I can eloquently and accurately explain my resume.

10. _____ I have a passion for the company that is interviewing me and the position I am applying for.

11. _____ I am prepared to be very positive in the interview.

12. _____ I can explain how I am a good time manager.

13. _____ I can provide examples of taking direction well.

14. _____ I can explain how I have a strong history of success.

15. _____ I can effectively communicate how the job I am interviewing for fits into my career plans.

16. _____ I have developed concise answers to the "Traditional Interview" sample questions.

17. _____ I have developed concise answers to the "Behavioral Interview" sample questions.

(continue to next page)

18. _____ I will find out what the next steps are in the interview process (i.e. another interview, job offer, etc.).

19. _____ I will find out when I will know the results of my interview.

20. _____ I will send a thank you letter to the interviewer.

In preparing for an interview, most people leave out one or more of these items. If you are able to check off each of these 20 things, you will be better prepared than most people for an interview. If there are certain things that you cannot check off, you should immediately do whatever is necessary to complete them. By completing this checklist before every interview, you will significantly increase the probability of getting the job of your choice.

CHAPTER 8

How Do I Pick the Right Company To Work For?

Choosing a Company To Work For

Once you have effectively researched job opportunities, developed a strong resume, and perfected your interview skills, you will begin to receive job offers. Sometimes you will get a call from employers indicating that they would like to hire you. However, most job offers are conveyed through either regular mail or email.

If you receive more than one job offer, you have an important decision to make. You must decide which job opportunity is the best one for you to accept at this time. All too often students take the first job offer they receive or the offer that pays the most. Unfortunately, these individuals often regret their hasty decision because they find themselves in jobs they don't like. There are ten things that you should consider when choosing a company to work for. These are:

1. Pay and benefits
2. The location of the job
3. The job responsibilities
4. Who you will report to
5. The real work hours
6. How the job fits into your career plans
7. The work environment
8. The culture of the organization
9. Visibility of the job
10. Promotion opportunities

We describe each of these considerations below. We also include five questions you should ask potential employers or co-workers about each of these considerations. You probably don't want to ask potential employers all of these questions. However, to make an informed job choice, you should ask many of these questions.

1. Pay and Benefits

Obviously, what the company is willing to pay you is an extremely important factor in your decision. Before you decide which job offer to accept, you should think about more than your weekly salary. You should consider your total compensation (salary and benefits). Some companies will pay high weekly salaries. However, their benefits package (vacation, sick days, health care, and retirement) is significantly less attractive than that of other companies.

If you are looking for a part-time job, then benefits will not be an important decision factor. It is also important to note that volunteer (nonpaying) jobs can provide valuable work experience that can lead to high paying jobs in the future. Consequently, you should not turn jobs down simply because of what they pay.

The five questions you should consider asking potential employers about pay and benefits are:

a) What is my annual/weekly pay?
b) How often will I receive a paycheck?
c) What benefits will I have?
d) What taxes will be taken out of my check?
e) What was the average pay increase for employees last year?

2. The Location of the Job

You should have thought about the plusses and minuses of the job location before deciding to interview in the first place. However, some job locations are better than others. Some great jobs may require you to take two buses to get to work while others may be in walking distance of your home. In addition, some jobs may require extensive travel. All too often students ignore the important transportation issues until it is too late.

The five questions you should consider asking about job location are:

a) Where will I spend most of my time and what are my work hours?
b) How much travel is required?
c) What are my transportation options?
d) Are their company-supported car pools?
e) Does the company allow telecommuting (working from home)?

---

3. The Job Responsibilities

Now that you have an offer, you can ask your potential employers some more detailed questions about the job you are considering. Position descriptions often gloss over important details of the job. You should find out what job responsibilities are most important. You should also learn about the evaluation process and criteria. The more you know about what measures of success exist for the job, the easier it will be to determine if the position is a good one for you.

The five questions you should consider asking about the job responsibilities are:

a) What is the primary responsibility of the position I have been offered?
b) What additional responsibilities will I have?
c) What are the measurable goals of the job?
d) What measures of success does the company use to evaluate employees?
e) How often will I be evaluated?

---

4. Who Will You Report To

Many human resources executives believe the saying "no one leaves a company, they only leave their boss." Your experience at an organization is directly related to the person (or people) you report to. A good boss who is friendly, supportive, encouraging, and concerned about your development will make the position wonderful. A bad boss who is negative, abusive, insecure, and demeaning will make the position a nightmare. It is very hard to determine whether a boss is good or bad by speaking to them. However, your potential co-workers will tell you whether it is a blessing or a curse working for certain people. You should therefore talk to potential co-workers before making a job choice.

The five questions you should consider asking about who you report to are:

a) Who will I report to directly?
b) Who else will be responsible for evaluating my performance?
c) May I speak with some employees that work for these individuals?
d) How long has my potential boss been with the company?
e) Have many people who have worked for this boss been promoted?

---

5. The Real Work Hours

Position descriptions typically list the official work hours. However, the "real" work hours frequently differ from those listed on the official paperwork. Some 9-am-to-5-pm jobs require you to work well beyond 5 pm to get your work done. Other jobs may provide flexibility in the work hours and require that you only stay until you get your work done. In addition, some jobs allow you to run errands during the work day while others force you to stay on site until the work day is over. You should find out as much as you can about the "real" work hours before you accept a position.

The five questions you should consider asking about work hours are:

a) What are my official work hours?
b) Does the company allow some flexibility in the work hours?
c) How much time is allowed for lunch?
d) What is the company policy regarding personal calls and Internet usage?
e) How late is the office open?

6. *How the Job Fits into Your Career Plans*

The benefit of determining your career interests before you interview is that you will have a better sense of the long-term benefits of a job offer. Your passion for the job you have is directly related to the career advancement opportunities it provides. Consequently, jobs that move you closer to your career goals are infinitely more interesting than those positions that don't help you with your career. You are more likely to succeed in career-related positions than in other positions. You should therefore choose the job that is a better fit with your career plans.

The five questions you should consider asking about how the job fits into your career plans are:

    a) **What career opportunities does this job lead to?**
    b) **What career-related skills will this position help me develop?**
    c) **What careers have other people in similar jobs pursued?**
    d) **Are there co-workers who can provide career advice?**
    e) **Are there any senior managers who will be willing to provide career advice?**

7. *The Work Environment*

Some work spaces are extremely uncomfortable. Employees frequently under-perform in these environments. Other work spaces are designed to create a positive environment that increases worker productivity. It is important that you compare different work environments before choosing a company.

You should pay attention to the office design, desk size, file space, bathroom accommodations, and cube or office size. Some people don't care about their work environment while others need to work in a certain type of office or location. The same thing applies if you are working in a retail location. Many people only want to work in a store or restaurant that is immaculate. Other people really don't care if the location is clean or dirty. Visit your potential work place to make sure that your work environment is acceptable before saying yes to an offer.

The five questions you should consider asking about the work environment if you are not able to visit the work location are:

a) Where will I be working?
b) Is there a receptionist by the front door?
c) Are the bathroom accommodations near my workspace?
d) Is there a lunch or snack room?
e) How old is the office?

---

8. *The Culture of the Organization*

Get a feel for the corporate culture of the organizations (and offices) that you are considering. Think of the culture as the environment, values, and style of an organization. If you don't feel comfortable in the organization's environment or don't share its values and style, you're going to have a difficult time succeeding there. It is extremely important to understand the "culture" of the organizations you are considering before choosing a company to work for because it is an important determinant of whether or not you will enjoy the job.

The culture of an organization is determined by the leadership style of the person in charge, how people interact with each other, who is promoted, and how people who are different are treated. Some organizations have a culture that is friendly and easy-going while other organizations have a very impersonal intensity. Many organizations welcome people with many different skills and backgrounds while others seek to promote people who are very much alike.

To learn about an organization's culture, you should speak with as many people as possible from the organization to get a sense of what they think the organization's culture is. You should make every effort to choose the company whose culture is the best fit with your personality.

The five questions you should consider asking about the culture of the organization are:

a) Does the company encourage competition or collaboration?
b) Are there senior managers who have a reputation as good mentors?

c) Does the company promote diversity at all levels?

d) How hard is it to find a sponsor (someone who will advocate for your promotion)?

e) Does the company encourage community service?

---

9. Visibility of the Job

If you are a hard worker, you should seek positions that have greater visibility in an organization. You should find a job where you will have frequent interaction with the senior managers of the organization. This interaction will enable decision makers to see how valuable you are to the organization and increase your chances for promotion or an increase in pay. Unfortunately, most jobs offered to students have no interaction with senior leaders. Consequently, there is little opportunity for rapid advancement or a significant increase in pay. The jobs with the greatest visibility are often the best.

The five questions you should consider asking about the visibility of the job are:

a) How much visibility does this job have within the organization?

b) What senior managers will I have a chance to interact with?

c) Does the company encourage interaction between staff at different levels?

d) Will I have a chance to work directly with the Chief Executive Officer (CEO)?

e) Will the people who supervise my boss have input into my evaluation?

---

10. Promotion Opportunities

One of the keys to having a successful work career is doing well in every position you hold. The best indication of success at work is getting a promotion. Even if you do not plan to remain at an organization, you should focus on doing well enough to get promoted. Your resume will be enhanced if you have been promoted in every position that you have held. Before deciding which job offer to take, you should determine what promotion opportunities are available for each job. You can do this by simply asking the human resources professional or the supervisor what opportunities for promotion exist in the position and how long does it typically take to get promoted. Obviously, jobs with many opportunities for promotion quickly are usually better than those that have few promotion opportunities.

The five questions you should consider asking about promotion opportunities are:

a) What promotion opportunities will be available to me?
b) Was the last person in this position promoted?
c) How often are promotions made?
d) What criteria is used to determine promotions?
e) How long does it typically take to get promoted?

RECOMMENDATION

There are many questionnaires designed to help individuals identify the right jobs and companies. You may find that completing a job questionnaire will force you to think in depth about different job factors. We have included a brief questionnaire that should help you decide what job factors are most important to you.

JOB PREFERENCE QUESTIONNAIRE

Rank in order of importance (1-15) the job factors that are important to you (with 1 being the most important):

A. _____ Gaining Experience

B. _____ Enhancing Career Opportunities

C. _____ Helping Others

D. _____ Working for a Good Boss

E. _____ Change and Variety

F. _____ Flexibility in Work Hours

G. _____ Comfortable Working Conditions

H. _____ Minimal Stress

I. _____ Prestige

J. _____ Moral Fulfillment

K. _____ Excitement

L. _____ Public Recognition

M. _____ Opportunity for Leadership

N. _____ Supportive Co-workers

O. _____ Recognition

You should complete this ranking to get a better idea of the types of jobs that are best suited to your personal interests. Once you have honestly prioritized these job factors, review the ten things that you should consider when choosing a company to work for. The best way to do this is to assign a weight to each of these ten things in the COMPANY COMPARISON WEIGHTING on the next page.

COMPANY COMPARISON WEIGHTING

It is important for you to compare the companies that have offered you a job. You should evaluate each offer by assigning a weight to each of the characteristics of a good job. The company that scores the highest is probably offering you the best job. Please weight each characteristic of a job offer below:

5 = Excellent
4 = Very Good
3 = Good
2 = Poor
1 = Unacceptable

A. _____ The pay and benefits

B. _____ The job location

C. _____ The job responsibilities

D. _____ The management ability of the people I will be reporting to

E. _____ The real work hours

F. _____ The fit with my career plans

G. _____ The work environment

H. _____ The culture of the organization

I. _____ The promotion opportunities the job provides

J. _____ The visibility of the job within the organization

You will find the comparison of companies using this unique weighting to be extremely useful. This weighting should help you choose which organization to work for. You may want to total the scores of each company in these areas and choose the company that has the highest score. Or, if some of these factors are more important than others, you may want to compare scores in those categories. For example, if pay and benefits, job location, and real work hours are the key factors in your decision, you should compare scores in these areas only.

SECTION II

Succeeding at Work

CHAPTER 9

Can I Learn To Manage My Time?

Learning How To Effectively Manage Time

Many students have difficulty managing their time because the concept is very new to them. They may have faced common deadlines like getting home for dinner or completing a homework assignment on time. However, they usually have not experienced the intense time pressure of work and life where deadlines often have severe negative consequences if they are not met (such as being fired).

Most jobs require strong time management skills. Employees need to manage their time in a way that allows them to get to work on time, complete their assignments ahead of time, and help their boss and co-workers complete their projects on time. In order to be successful at work and life, you must effectively manage your time.

To do this, you should be aware of the following three things:

1. Basics of Time Management
2. Common Myths About Time Management
3. Advanced Time Management

1. Basics of Time Management

Most people have heard of the concept of time management. However, they think that it simply means that you get to places on time. However, there are some important basics of time management that you should know to begin the process of developing the ability to effectively manage your time. These are:

a) Understand the value of time.
b) Learn how to set time-based goals.
c) Know the consequences of missing deadlines.
d) Learn how to avoid wasting time.
e) Practice time management skills.

Understand the Value of Time

The saying "Wisdom is wasted on the old" is often true. Typically, the older a person gets, the more they realize that time is the most valuable thing in the world. If you do not have time, you cannot do anything. Unfortunately, many students think that they will live forever and that they have plenty of time to do anything that they want to do when they want to do it. They therefore do not make a special effort to plan their time or treasure the valuable time that they have.

Unfortunately, the careers like law and medicine, that require graduate education, mandate that you are intensely focused on these careers in high school or at a minimum as a freshman in college. You do not have time to waste by neglecting your school work. You also cannot afford to violate the law because a mark on your record can severely limit your career options. The top medical, law, and business schools look for well-rounded students who have outstanding grades, unique extracurricular experience, and exceptional work experience.

It is a good idea to begin to make an effort to understand the value of your time no later than your senior year in high school. Young people with special areas of focus (i.e. athletes, musicians, and scholars) learn very early in life about the value of time. They discover that the only way to excel is to schedule their day around practice. They learn that to achieve a goal, they must value their time. If you are serious about succeeding at work and life, you must begin to understand the value of time.

Learn How To Set Time-Based Goals

It is very easy to set goals. However, it is extremely difficult to set achievable goals with realistic timetables. It is even harder to achieve these goals. The most common mistake that people make is that they do not set any goals at all. They go through life without real focus and direction. They live hour by hour with no real plan and are often unhappy with their career and life.

The second most common mistake that people make is that they set unrealistic goals with unrealistic timetables. They create daily "To Do" lists that list more activities than they could possibly accomplish in a day. They therefore never complete the list and feel that they have been unproductive. Successful individuals have learned how to prioritize their goals by time.

Know the Consequences of Missing Deadlines

The primary reason that many students do not develop strong time management skills is that they typically do not face severe consequences for missing deadlines. They often don't lose anything for being late or missing a deadline. Unfortunately, the consequences of missing deadlines in the world of work can be very severe depending on the situation.

There is no acceptable excuse for being late to a job interview. Consequently, being late for an interview usually means you will not receive a job offer. Being late to work multiple times without a good excuse often means that you will be fired from a job. Not fulfilling a promise to complete a work project by a certain date can have very different consequences. If it is a small project that is not central to your job responsibilities, then the consequences will probably not be severe. However, if it is a major project that is central to your position, then the punishment could be anything from a bad evaluation to being fired.

Everyone, at one time or another, misses deadlines. However, once you think that you may not make a deadline, you should immediately contact your supervisors to let them know that you may be delayed and keep them in the loop about your progress. People do not like negative surprises. The fewer of these surprises you provide, the better. Make sure that you are aware of all of the consequences of missing deadlines at work and in life.

Learn How to Avoid Wasting Time

It is amazingly easy to waste time. Society's technological advances have helped to increase personal and work productivity. However, these advances have also made it easier than ever to waste time. The volume of information on the Internet and the quality and quantity of video games and other technological temptations make it easy for you to avoid doing required work. To avoid wasting time, you must know the difference between "work time" (when you are working on work-related projects) and "play time" (your free time). This distinction may seem obvious. However, many people waste valuable work time playing games or pursuing unproductive Internet searches. To ensure that you will be successful at work, you have to develop the personal discipline to focus on work during work time and games and other activities during play time.

Practice Time Management Skills

Remember "Practice makes perfect." The only way to effectively manage your time is by practicing time management skills. You should begin by reconfirming your long-term goals. The most effective time managers know what their long-term objectives are and develop time-sensitive goals that will help them achieve these objectives.

Once you have reconfirmed your long-term goals (1 year, 5 years and 10 years) and written them down, you should organize a "3-D To Do List." This is a three-dimensional list where you have the goals that have to be completed today in the "1st Dimension" on one page. You place the goals that need to be completed in three days in the "2nd Dimension" on a second page. Finally, you place the goals that need to be completed in a week in the "3rd Dimension" on a third page. Once an item has been completed, you should draw a line through it. If the item has not been completed in the specified time period, then you circle it (for inclusion on a future list). If an item should be taken off of the list, you put an "X" through it.

By developing these lists for both work and home, you will begin to accomplish more in a shorter period of time. In addition, you will learn more about the value of time and develop the ability to be an excellent time manager.

---

2. Common Myths About Time Management

There are many common myths about time management. Bookstores are filled with "How To" books that supposedly help you manage your time and your life in several easy steps. The reality is that learning to manage your time is not easy. It takes hard work and a dedicated focus on setting goals and understanding time constraints. Unfortunately, there are some common myths about time management that you should know about before you focus on advanced time management.

The five biggest myths about time management are:

a) **Planning your time takes more time.**
b) **A time management problem means that there is simply not enough time.**
c) **The busier you are, the better you use your time.**
d) **If you feel rushed, you are not managing your time well.**
e) **You get more done when you use sugar, coffee, or something else to keep you awake.**

Planning Your Time Takes More Time

Many people believe that taking time to plan their day around their goals slows them down. They believe that the time it takes to plan could be better used actually doing something. They therefore do not take the time necessary to effectively plan their time around short-term and long-term goals. However, they do not realize that it is a common myth that planning your time takes more time. The opposite is true.

You are much more productive if you take the time to plan how you will use your time. This important planning helps you to organize your time in a way that will enable you to more effectively accomplish your goals. However, you can only plan your time effectively if you know what your goals are. You should therefore take the time to set specific measurable short- and long-term goals and plan your time in a way that will help you reach these goals.

A Time Management Problem Means That There Is Simply Not Enough Time

People who are very busy often feel that their time management problems are caused by a shortage of time. They feel that they are not accomplishing what they want to accomplish because there simply is not enough time to do what they think they need to do. Frequently, these individuals feel this way because they are not setting effective time-based goals. They are often wasting a lot of time on unproductive activities that will not help them achieve their goals. They feel rushed because they have unrealistic expectations about their ability to complete tasks.

The old adage "a crazy person is someone who does the same thing over and over but expects a different result" often applies to people who feel that there is never enough time to do what they want to do. Day after day, they feel that they are in a time crunch. However, they never change their approach to time management but expect things to change. If you feel that there is never enough time, you should take time to review your goals and the time you have set aside to accomplish these goals and change one or both of them. You should either have fewer goals or increase the estimated time it will take to reach them.

The Busier You Are, the Better You Use Your Time

The old saying "if you want someone to get things done, find a busy person" is often true. However, it is inaccurate to assume that just because some people are busy, they are using their time well. Frequently, very busy people are working "hard" but not "smart." They may be doing a lot of things that keep them busy. However, they are not working strategically. Many people waste valuable time making copies, searching the Internet, or having unproductive conversations at work instead of doing what they need to do to achieve their goals. In addition, many people are focused on doing what they think is urgent and not what is necessary.

You must develop the ability to prioritize your activities and determine the complexity of a task. Typically, the more complex a task, the sooner

106

you should start working on it. Many people wait until the last minute to begin working on complex projects. They therefore find themselves swamped with work shortly before the project is completed. Consequently, they are very busy because of a poor use of their time. You should always focus on completing the most difficult tasks as soon as possible so you are not busier than you need to be.

If You Feel Rushed, You Are Not Managing Your Time Well

Many people incorrectly assume that if you are a good time manager, you will never feel rushed. Unfortunately, the often last-minute demands of work may make you feel rushed even if you manage your time well. The key in determining whether you are managing your time well is if you are working toward one or more of your goals. You may frequently feel rushed as you spend time attempting to achieve these goals. If you are not spending your time working toward your goals, you are probably not managing your time well (whether or not you are feeling rushed). Good time managers are focused on achieving their goals on time (not whether or not they are feeling rushed).

You Get More Done When You Use Something To Keep You Awake

College students often brag about the number of times they have stayed up all night to complete a school assignment. They treat these "all-nighters" as a badge of honor. They frequently tell stories of drinking coffee or eating chocolate bars to keep them awake so that they can complete their work. Unfortunately, what they don't know is that, no matter how productive they feel, they did not do their best work during these hours. Unfortunately, no matter what you take to keep awake, your mind will be tired and much less effective than it would have been after a good night's sleep. In addition, substances that keep you awake force you to hit a mental wall sooner or later that inhibits your ability to think effectively.

One of the secrets to effective time management is getting sufficient sleep. You would never think about running a marathon without sufficient exercise and rest. Likewise, you should never think about effective time management without sufficient rest. Usually people who have to stay up late to complete a school or work assignment are doing so because they have not managed their time well. If they had been good time managers, they could have avoided these "all-nighters." To effectively manage your time, you should make every effort to get a good night's sleep every evening.

---

3. Advanced Time Management

Once you have learned the basics and the key myths about time management, you are ready to focus on advanced time management. Fortunately, most people understand the importance of time management. However, few people make the effort to become good time managers. They focus on completing their work on time. However, because they are not proactive in their efforts to manage time, they find themselves constantly reacting to situations. They are not in control of their time. Instead, they are letting time manage them.

There are five simple techniques to manage your time more efficiently. These are:

a) **Write down your long-term goals.**
b) **Set a realistic timetable for each goal.**
c) **Develop a system to reward your progress toward these goals.**
d) **Write a realistic "To Do" list every day.**
e) **Permanently record your major accomplishments.**

Write Down Your Long-Term Goals

The key to effective time management is setting long-term goals that you are passionate about achieving. If you do not take the time to set specific measurable long-term goals, you have no idea how to use your time effectively. You find yourself doing things without purpose or direction. You should begin the goal-setting process by establishing measurable long-term personal and work goals.

You should start with the long-term goals because they will be the foundation of your intermediate and short-term goals. You should write your long-term personal and work goals on paper. Your long-term goals should be based on what you are most interested in achieving at work and in life. Don't limit the initial list to what you think is possible. List all the things that you dreamed of accomplishing in life and work over the next 5, 10, or 20 years. Each of these goals should be something you are passionate about. They should also be difficult to achieve. Some of these goals may be unrealistic. However, list them anyway. Even if they are not achievable, similar goals that are less challenging may be possible. We will determine how realistic these goals are when we determine the timeframe for achieving these goals below.

Set a Realistic Timetable for Each Goal

If you have enough time, you can achieve anything. Unfortunately, we do not have enough time to do everything that we want to do. Time determines whether our goals are realistic or not. Now that you have written down your long-term goals, you should begin assigning realistic timeframes for each of these goals. If you are a senior in college with a "C" average, it is unrealistic to set a goal of being Valedictorian of your college class since most of these individuals have "A" averages. However, if you are a senior in high school with a "C" average, you may be able to be the Valedictorian of your senior class in college if you are willing to work extremely hard and attend a school that will enable you to excel academically.

You should estimate how long it takes to accomplish each of these goals based on how long it has taken other people to achieve the same goal. If you discover that you will never have enough time to accomplish this long-term goal, you should take the goal off the list. This is sometimes a painful process. It may force you to come to the realization that you will never be a star professional athlete or President of the United States. However, it will help you focus on other goals that are equally as important to you.

Once you have completed your list of long-term goals with clear timetables, you should begin to list your intermediate and short-term goals. These goals should be things that you have to accomplish before you can achieve your long-term goals. For example, if you want to be a doctor, then you should set an intermediate goal of graduating from medical school and completing your residency. You should also set a short-term goal of getting excellent grades in school. Like your long-term goals, intermediate and short-term goals should also have specific timeframes associated with them. Once these goals are set, you should develop a system to reward your progress toward these goals.

Develop a System To Reward Your Progress Toward These Goals

Ignoring the need for a personal reward system is one of the major mistakes that people make when setting goals. We assume that achieving a goal is enough of a reward. However, most people need special incentives to motivate them to do what is necessary to achieve a goal. If personal and work goals are set properly, they will be difficult to achieve. They will frequently require great personal sacrifice.

To inspire you to make the sacrifices necessary to continue to achieve your goals, you should establish a reward system that is meaningful to you. The reward could be as simple as treating yourself (and possibly your family) to dinner or a movie. It could be going on an elaborate trip or simply taking the day off. The key is that the reward should be comparable to the achievement. If you have accomplished a minor goal, then your reward may be something small. However, if you have achieved a major goal, then the reward should be a significant one. This type of reward system will motivate you to work harder than ever on the next personal goal.

Write a Realistic "To Do" List Every Day

Once you have set realistic time-based goals and established a meaningful reward system, you are ready to establish a daily "To Do" list system. As discussed earlier, you should develop a "3-D To Do List." This is the three-dimensional list where you have the goals that have to be completed today in the "1st Dimension" on one page, the goals that need to be completed in three days in the "2nd Dimension" on a second page, and the goals that need to be completed in a week in the "3rd Dimension" on a third page. Once an item has been completed, you should draw a line through it. If the item has not been completed in the specified time period, then you circle it and move it to the appropriate list. If an item should be taken off the list, you put an "X" through it.

Once you develop an effective system to create the "3D To Do List," you will maximize the amount of time you are spending each day working toward your long-term goals. In addition, you will begin to accomplish more in a shorter period of time, learn more about the value of time, and develop the ability to be an excellent time manager. Unfortunately, it will take you several weeks before you feel comfortable with this system. However, once you have mastered this system, you will find that work and life are much more enjoyable.

Permanently Record Your Major Accomplishments

People who are experienced time managers discover that they have a tendency to move on immediately after accomplishing a goal. Even if they have developed an effective personal reward system, they often forget how difficult it was to achieve a goal. It is therefore extremely important for people to keep a permanent record of their accomplishments. Some people use plastic sheets in binders to keep documents that symbolize their accomplishments. Other people frame these documents. Still others keep a diary of their accomplishments.

Unfortunately, pursuing challenging goals is often difficult. There will be times when you want to give up on your goal. However, your record of past accomplishments will help to motivate you to achieve your goal. Often, a reminder that you have overcome similar challenges motivates you to successfully face new challenges. Success in life and work is often based on the belief that you can succeed. Documenting your past accomplishments can give you the confidence to succeed.

RECOMMENDATION

Most students do not understand how important it is to learn how to manage their time. They do not know that effective time management skills will give them greater control over both their career and their life. As a student focused on success, you should begin practicing time management techniques as soon as possible so that you can develop these skills early in your career. One way to assess your time management skills is to complete the TIME MANAGEMENT QUESTIONNAIRE on the next page.

TIME MANAGEMENT QUESTIONNAIRE

This questionnaire will help you determine if you are doing everything that you can to effectively manage your time. Please answer the time management questions below by circling either *Yes* or *No*.

1. Do you understand the value of time? **Yes   No**

2. Do you set time-based goals? **Yes   No**

3. Do you understand the consequences
    of missing deadlines? **Yes   No**

4. Do you know how to avoid wasting time? **Yes   No**

5. Do you practice your time management skills? **Yes   No**

6. Do you write down your long-term goals? **Yes   No**

7. Do you set realistic timetables for each goal? **Yes   No**

8. Do you develop a goal-based reward system? **Yes   No**

9. Do you write down a realistic "To Do" list
    every day? **Yes   No**

10. Do you keep a permanent record of your
    major accomplishments? **Yes   No**

This TIME MANAGEMENT QUESTIONNAIRE will help you determine how effectively you manage your time. If you answered "Yes" to each of these questions, then you have done an outstanding job of managing your time. However, if you answered "No" to one or more of these questions, you should work on those aspects of time management until you can accurately answer "Yes" to every question. This exercise will significantly increase the probability that you are managing your time well.

CHAPTER 10

What Are Ethics and Why Are They Important?

Ethical and Moral Beliefs

The headlines are filled with stories of business executives, politicians, and celebrities who have broken the law or stretched the boundaries of morality and ethics. Almost every week, we hear about business executives who manipulated earnings reports to make money, politicians who lie to win an election, movie stars who are hooked on drugs, and athletes who take illegal performance-enhancing substances to excel in a sport. The unfortunate message that many students get from these stories is that you should do whatever it takes to succeed as long as you don't get caught. Nothing could be farther from the truth.

The only individuals who succeed in the long run are those who live their lives based on ethical and moral beliefs developed from their life experiences. These individuals are able to resist the temptation to violate common business and personal ethics. You almost never read about them because they succeed without publicity.

To be successful in business and life, you should know the answers to the following three questions about ethics:

1. What are ethics?
2. Why are they important?
3. What can I do to improve my ethical behavior?

1. What Are Ethics?

The Miriam-Webster Dictionary defines *ethics* as "moral principles or practice." The dictionary defines *moral* as "of or relating to principles of right or wrong." Ethics can therefore be considered the practice of doing the right thing. Many people try to justify unethical behavior that they think will help them achieve their goals when, in fact, it will prevent them from achieving their long-term goals. Unfortunately, many students are never taught the basics of ethical behavior.

The five key components of ethical behavior are:

a) Following the "Golden Rule"
b) Telling the truth
c) Respecting property that is not your own
d) Avoiding conflicts of interest
e) Helping others

Following the "Golden Rule"

The best way to ensure that your behavior is ethical is to follow the "Golden Rule." This rule says: "Treat others as you want to be treated." This simple phrase provides a powerful guide to behaving ethically. Unfortunately, most people ignore this rule and frequently treat others inappropriately. Before you take an action that will impact someone else, you should take time to ask yourself "if this happened to me, how would I feel about it?" If you honestly answer this question, then you will know exactly what you should do.

Telling the Truth

Many people have become accustomed to doing whatever is easier in the short-term. They rarely think about the long-term consequences of their words and deeds. Lying is often the easiest thing to do in the short-term. These people therefore find themselves frequently telling lies. They get away with these lies in the short-term. However, the long-term consequences of lying can often be disastrous. For example, if your boss asks you if you are almost finished with a project, you may tell her that you are almost done when you are actually far from done. Hearing that you are almost finished with the project, she may make the deadline earlier than originally planned because she believed you. You will therefore not be able to complete it on time and at minimum disappoint your boss. You may even get fired because of this lie (which you may have thought was a relatively minor untruth). In short, you should always tell the truth (even when it is harder than lying).

Respecting Property That Is Not Your Own

Most people think that theft only applies when a valuable object is stolen. They don't believe that taking office supplies or inappropriately using equipment is theft. However, theft can be defined as simply "taking or using property that is not your own for unauthorized use or sale." In the work place, people frequently steal property because they do not respect company property. They believe that because they work for an organization, the organization's property is their own. Nothing could be farther from the truth.

Obviously, taking pens and pencils for personal use is overlooked by most organizations. However, some employees graduate from taking pens to taking staplers to taking reams of paper to taking computers. Many end up in prison because they became addicted to theft. In addition, making copies of personal items without permission or playing games on your work computer without permission are considered theft as well.

Virtually everyone knows that it is unethical to steal. However, peer pressure often motivates people to participate in theft. Whenever you are tempted to take something from work or someone else, you should ask yourself the simple question: "Am I taking or using something that belongs to me or someone else?"

Avoiding Conflicts of Interest

Determining whether you have a conflict of interest is not as easy as determining whether you are lying or stealing. A conflict of interest occurs when your personal interests or outside activities interfere with your ability to effectively perform your job or act in the interest of your employer. For example, if Company A and B sell the same product and regularly compete with each other, then it is a conflict of interest for you to get paid to sell products for both companies. You have to choose which company to work for and sell their products.

You must not knowingly place yourself in a position that would appear to conflict with the interest of the company. It is also unethical to engage in freelance activity that will impact on the time that you have for your job or the quality of work you are performing for your employer. Unethical conflicts of interest can obviously take place in your personal life. If you have a girlfriend or boyfriend, it is obviously a conflict of interest to date someone else. Before engaging in any activity outside of your job or relationship, you should ask yourself: "Does this activity conflict in any way with my job or relationship?"

Helping Others

Ethical behavior includes the act of helping other people. To truly behave in an ethical manner, you should, at a minimum, help others in distress. For example, if a co-worker is struggling with an assignment and you have the time and ability to help, you should. Frequently, these types of favors are returned (this person or someone else will help you when you are having a problem). However, even if this favor is not returned, helping others is the appropriate and ethical thing to do.

---

2. Why Are Ethics Important?

There are five reasons why ethical behavior is important. These are because it . . .

a) is the right thing to do.
b) simplifies your life.
c) maximizes your chances of success.
d) helps you feel better.
e) makes your world a better place.

Behaving Ethically Is the Right Thing To Do

Most people know the difference between right and wrong. They recognize that they should not hurt people or steal property and that they should be polite, honest, and helpful. However, frequently they do what they know they should not because doing the wrong thing is often easier. They want to get something quickly so they lie and steal. They want to succeed so they are selfish or rude to others. Most of the individuals that do these things know that they are wrong; however, they do unethical things anyway.

Unfortunately, unethical behavior is addictive. Once you get in the habit of being unethical, it is hard to return to a pattern of ethical behavior. This unethical behavior often forces people's lives to spiral out of control. They end up in prison, addicted to drugs, or even dead. To avoid this suffering, you should make every effort to behave ethically simply because it is the right thing to do.

Ethical Behavior Simplifies Your Life

One of the biggest benefits of behaving ethically is that it simplifies your life. In the long run, lying is much more difficult than telling the truth. Lies grow exponentially. You cannot tell just one. You have to remember what lie you told to whom. For example, if you told John one lie and Sue another lie and Jane yet another lie, you have to remember what you told each of them. However, if you told the same truth to John, Sue, and Jane, then you only have to remember the truth. In addition, by following the "Golden Rule," you have a clear guide as to how you should treat other people. Life is so much simpler when you behave ethically.

Ethical Behavior Maximizes Your Chances of Success

Success in life almost always occurs because of the help of other people. To get promoted at work or find the love of your life, you need help from other people. One of the biggest mistakes that students make at work is that they think that they can do everything themselves. They do not understand that their success is largely dependent on the relationships that they make at work. Their interaction with their boss and co-workers is the single most important determinant of their success or failure at work. Likewise, many love connections come about because of friends introducing two people. If individuals are known to have questionable ethics, then other people will not recommend that they get promoted at work or that they meet a friend who could be a possible love connection.

Behaving Ethically Helps You Feel Better

Very few people think about the tremendous stress caused by behaving unethically. As mentioned previously, keeping up with one's inappropriate behavior (like lies) can be extremely difficult. Remembering what you said to whom is extremely stressful. Stealing or misusing company property causes tremendous stress because you will always be worried about getting caught. However, behaving ethically has the opposite effect. When you are committed to behaving ethically, you do not deal with the stress of lying or stealing. You feel great about life because you have the respect of your friends and co-workers and have a clear understanding of right and wrong that will guide you in every situation.

Ethical Behavior Makes Your World a Better Place

The biggest problem with behaving unethically comes when your friends or co-workers don't trust you because of your unethical behavior. Losing the confidence of people who you spend considerable time with can make your life miserable. People will not confide in you because they can't trust you. You may find yourself spending time with people with questionable ethics because those individuals with strong ethics will avoid spending time with you.

In contrast, the most rewarding thing about behaving ethically is that you gain the admiration of co-workers, friends, and family. When you develop a reputation as someone who is known for their commitment to behaving ethically and responsibly, you gain tremendous respect from the people you interact with. The old adage "people are judged by the company they keep" is very true. You will spend more time with people who have a strong sense of ethics. Your world will be a better place because you will receive greater work and personal opportunities because of the quality of people you are interacting with.

---

3. What Can I Do To Improve My Ethical Behavior?

There are five things that you should do to improve your ethical behavior. These are:

a) Define how you want to be treated.
b) Practice telling the truth.
c) Put yourself in other people's shoes.
d) Learn how to value property.
e) Try to make life better for other people.

Define How You Want To Be Treated

Before you can follow the "Golden Rule" and treat people the way you want to be treated, you should take time to think about how you would like people to treat you. You should write down the ten most important ways you would like to be treated. The list could include your desire for people to listen to you, tell you the truth, respect you, etc. Once you have completed this list, then you will have a good idea how you should treat others.

Practice Telling the Truth

Clearly, one of the most unethical things that you can do is tell a lie. However, for many people, telling the truth is not natural. It is very easy to tell one lie. However, as previously mentioned, once you tell one lie, you will find yourself forced to tell several other lies in order to justify your first lie. You should therefore practice telling the truth always. However, it is essential that you, at a minimum, practice telling the truth in every work situation. This may sound like an easy thing to do. However, sometimes telling the truth is extremely difficult because people often do not want to hear the truth. You should make a personal commitment to tell the truth in every possible work situation regardless of what you think the outcome will be. The more that you practice doing this, the more successful you will be telling the truth in every situation at home and at work.

Put Yourself in Other People's Shoes

Most people do not take the time to think about other people's perspectives. They are focused on their personal needs and frequently disregard the needs and perspectives of others. To enhance your ethical behavior, it is extremely important for you to take time to consider how other people feel. It is especially critical for you to think about a person's reaction before you do or say something that will affect them.

By taking a moment to do this type of reflection, you can restate your words or redesign your actions in a way that will be mutually beneficial. For example, if someone asks you to review a work or school document that they have prepared that needs significant revision, you should think how the person would feel about your constructive criticism. If this person is especially sensitive about criticism, then you can rephrase your comments in a way that will not offend them. You might say something like "you have a real talent for writing. Other than the following revisions (list them), this document is excellent." This comment will give them confidence about their abilities and inspire them to make the necessary changes. By taking time to put yourself in other people's shoes, you will develop a reputation as an ethical co-worker or friend.

Learn How To Value Property

It is quite common for people to place great value on their own property and devalue other people's property. All too often, people misuse or steal company property without thinking twice. However, they are extremely careful with their own property. Employees often justify scratching, dropping, breaking, and stealing company property by stating that their company has plenty of money to repair the damage or buy new property. A company's financial capabilities are no excuse for misusing their property. It is unethical to intentionally damage property that is not your own. To enhance your ethical behavior, you should adopt a "Golden Property Rule" where you treat other people's property as you would want them to treat your own property.

Try To Make Life Better for Other People

It is not enough to do the right thing only with your friends and the people you work or go to school with. Those individuals who take their ethical behavior very seriously will try to make life better for people who they do not know. If you are serious about succeeding in work and life, you should do the same. Volunteering your time to feed the hungry, help the homeless, or serve on a civic sector board will give you a perspective on life that is extremely valuable. You will understand how fortunate you are and develop a greater appreciation for your life. The opportunity to help others combined with this newfound appreciation for life should make you happier and inspire you to work even harder at becoming successful in everything that you do.

RECOMMENDATION

You should take the time to understand how important it is to behave ethically. Your reputation is the most valuable thing that you own. A great reputation can lead to success at work and in life. A bad reputation can keep you from getting a job and ruin your life. Your reputation is based on your morals, honesty, and compassion for others. You should do everything that you can to develop a reputation as someone with the highest ethical principles. One way to ensure that you have the highest ethical principles is to complete each of the items on the ETHICS CHECKLIST on the next page.

ETHICS CHECKLIST

The list below contains many of the things that you should do to improve your ethical behavior. Please check each of the items that you have completed below:

1. _____ I have learned why ethics are important.

2. _____ I have learned how ethical behavior can improve my life and career.

3. _____ I define on paper how I want to be treated.

4. _____ I try to "put myself in other people's shoes" to understand their perspective.

5. _____ I follow the "Golden Rule."

6. _____ I try my best to tell the truth.

7. _____ I respect other people's property.

8. _____ I avoid conflicts of interest.

9. _____ I go out of my way to support other people.

10. _____ I do what I can to help others improve their ethical behavior.

By completing each of the ten things on this checklist, you demonstrate your commitment to behaving ethically. If there are items that you are not able to check off because you have not done them, you should do them as soon as possible. You will enhance your chances of success in a career and life if you do each of the things on the ETHICS CHECKLIST.

CHAPTER 11

Why Is Dressing for Success Important?

Dressing for Success

Many students do not understand the difference between dressing for success and dressing to impress their friends. To impress their friends, they will frequently wear the most popular, informal clothing available. Unfortunately, these informal styles are inappropriate for most work places. To dress for success, students must wear the highest quality clothing in the most popular styles for that place of work. Once you receive a job offer, you should find out what the dress code is. You should determine what the best-dressed people at this place of work wear. In some offices, dressing for success may require that you wear a suit every day. You should therefore buy as many high quality suits as you can afford. Other work locations will allow you to wear jeans. You should therefore wear the best jeans you can afford.

No matter what type of clothing you are required to wear at work, there are five keys to dressing for success. These are:

    A. Keep your clothes neat, clean, and wrinkle-free.
    B. Ensure that your shoes are in good condition.
    C. Make sure that your hair is combed or styled.
    D. Keep your clothes and make-up subtle.
    E. Always stand up straight and walk with pride.

Most people do not understand that dressing for success plays an important role in determining whether or not they are successful in a job. There are ten main reasons why dressing for success is important to your career. These are:

1. First impressions are lasting.
2. You show your commitment.
3. Image is everything.
4. You will have greater confidence.
5. Professionalism is the key to work success.
6. Presence is important.
7. You gain the respect of others.
8. People assume that you are intelligent.
9. You will be able to interact with more successful people.
10. You will have more opportunity.

---

1. First Impressions Are Lasting

Unfortunately, people make long-term determinations about others based on their initial impressions. If the first impression is positive, then people make favorable assumptions about a person. If the first impression is negative, then people make unfavorable assumptions about a person. For example, if a student comes to work with wrinkled casual clothes, a manager will likely assume that the student is not a hard worker and does not care about appearance or the job. However, if a student comes to work wearing neat and clean professional clothes, then they will assume that the student cares about appearance, is a hard worker, and wants to succeed in the job. It is very hard to change first impressions, so make a special effort to dress for success so that your first impression is a positive one.

---

2. You Show Your Commitment

By dressing for success, you are demonstrating that you are willing to make an investment in yourself for the job. Most employers understand that students and recent graduates are more comfortable wearing casual clothing. They take special notice of those students who are well dressed in business attire because of the commitment they are making to the job and the organization.

---

3. Image Is Everything

No matter what you do at work, you will develop an image in the mind of your co-workers. This image can be a very good one or a very bad one. Unfortunately, people like to classify others into certain categories. This is often unfair. However, it is a reality of the world. If someone is late a few times to work, that person will frequently be categorized as being "always late." That person will quickly develop an image (which may not be true) as someone who is late, does not take the job seriously, and is unlikely to be employed for long. Likewise, if someone is always well dressed and a does a good job at work, that person will be categorized as a "fast tracker" (someone who will be extremely successful and will get promoted quickly). It is therefore extremely important to dress for success to enhance your image at work.

---

4. You Will Have Greater Confidence

What you wear will impact your confidence. If you dress for success, you will be more confident because you know that you are looking as good as you possibly can. This internal confidence will show in the way you walk and speak. People will recognize this confidence and compliment you more often. These compliments will give you even more confidence. Dressing for success can therefore increase your confidence exponentially.

---

5. Professionalism Is the Key to Work Success

The key to success in the work place is professionalism. You must recognize that having a job is serious business. All too often students do not take their job very seriously. They speak and dress in a very informal manner that can sometimes turn off their boss and co-workers. By dressing for success, you will naturally behave in a more professional manner. You will feel like a professional with an intense focus on success. The professional demeanor that comes from dressing for success will help you succeed at work.

---

6. Presence Is Important

To dress for success, you must do more than wear nice clothes. You must stand up straight and walk with confidence and purpose. By doing this, you develop a work presence that can be extremely impressive to others. Your managers and co-workers will respond to you in a very positive way if you present a total package of quality clothes, excellent posture, and a purposeful walk. You should focus on developing a strong presence because it can help you get a promotion or raise.

---

7. You Gain the Respect of Others

By dressing for success, people will take notice of you. They will have greater respect for you as a person and the work that you do in the office. They will give you the benefit of the doubt when you are working with them. They are also more likely to introduce you to key people because of their respect for you. These introductions can help you get promoted, receive a raise, or get an incredible new job offer. Respect in the work place is hard to get. However, once you have the respect of others, there will be many new and exciting job prospects presented to you. Dressing for success is the first step in gaining the respect of supervisors and co-workers.

---

8. People Assume That You Are Intelligent

Clearly, just because you dress well does not mean that you are intelligent. However, unbelievably, many people assume that well-dressed people are smarter than poorly dressed people. By dressing for success, people will assume that you are intelligent and give you more exciting work assignments. If you do not dress well, you are likely to get the most boring assignments available. It is not fair. However, it is the way some offices operate. To increase your chances of being given interesting job assignments, you should dress for success.

9. You Will Be Able To Interact with More Successful People

The confidence and respect that emanates from dressing for success will increase your interaction with successful people. Successful managers will be drawn to you because of this confidence and respect. You will be invited to participate in activities (meetings, lunches, outings, etc.) that are not available to other people (who have not taken the time to dress for success). During these activities, you will have a chance to show these successful individuals how committed you are to your job and that you should get a raise and be promoted. This interaction with successful people will also give you exposure to careers that you otherwise might never know about. Never underestimate the power of dressing for success.

10. You Will Have More Opportunity

No matter what career you decide to pursue, dressing for success will play an important role in helping you succeed. As described previously, your clothes will help you make a positive impression, show your commitment to the job, enhance your image, increase your confidence, demonstrate professionalism, establish a strong presence, gain the respect of others, convince people of your intelligence, and enable you to interact with more successful people. However, the most important benefit of dressing for success is that it will significantly increase the opportunities that you have to succeed in a career. The positive aura that surrounds well-dressed people leads to pay increases, promotions, and networking opportunities that serve as the foundation of a successful career. You should make every effort to dress for success because what you wear can play an important role in hurting or helping your career.

RECOMMENDATION

Dressing for success can play an extremely important role in your career growth. What you wear can stimulate you internally by increasing your confidence and self-respect. It can also motivate the people around you to do positive things for you. Consequently, you should do everything that you can to be the best-dressed person (by the standards of your workplace) at your job. One of the most effective ways to determine your primary reasons for dressing for success is to complete the DRESS FOR SUCCESS RANKING on the next page.

DRESS FOR SUCCESS RANKING

To determine your personal reasons for dressing for success, rank the ten reasons to dress for success (1-10) in order of importance to you (1 being most important) below:

A. _____ To make a good first impression.

B. _____ To show my commitment to succeeding at work.

C. _____ To enhance my image.

D. _____ To have more confidence about my abilities.

E. _____ To look more professional.

F. _____ To have greater presence.

G. _____ To ensure that my co-workers have more respect for me.

H. _____ To increase the likelihood that people will think that I am intelligent.

I. _____ To interact with more successful people.

J. _____ To have more opportunities to succeed.

By ranking the reasons to dress for success, you should be inspired to dress and behave in a way that generates the benefits that interest you the most. For example, if you want a greater presence at work, you will dress, walk, and behave in a way that enhances the manner in which you interact with others. Likewise, to show your commitment to succeeding at work, you will not only dress well, you will go above and beyond the call of duty to do a good job on your projects at work.

CHAPTER 12

If I Don't Have a Car, How Do I Get To Work?

The Importance of Transportation

Unfortunately, one of the main reasons that students are not able to accept or keep good jobs is that they do not have adequate transportation. For many students, transportation to and from work is rarely a problem. They may have a car, live in an area where there are many available jobs, or have access to plenty of public transportation. They therefore do not have to limit their job search because of transportation limitations. However, many students are not so fortunate. They may live in areas with few jobs and transportation options. Unfortunately, these students often miss out on some great jobs because they limit their job search without fully researching their transportation options. In addition, some students take jobs knowing that they will have trouble getting to and from work on time. They are frequently fired because of their inability to consistently get to work on time. It is therefore extremely important for you to think about your transportation options before accepting a position.

Assuming that you do not have a car, the five key steps you must take to ensure that transportation does not keep you from getting (or succeeding in) a new job are:

1. Identify realistic transportation options provided by friends and family.
2. Thoroughly review your public transportation options.
3. Honestly assess the reliability of each mode of public transportation.
4. Identify job opportunities that are easily reached by available transportation.
5. Identify job opportunities that provide transportation.

---

1. Family and Friends Transportation Options

Finding a job is one of the most important things that high school or college students can do. By working, students learn many of the skills necessary to succeed at work, in school, and in life. Consequently, it is very important that family members and friends support the efforts of students to get and keep a job. One of the most important ways that family members can help students succeed at work is by ensuring that they get to work on time and get home at a reasonable hour. All too often, students are reluctant to ask family members and friends if they could help them get to and from work. However, once you have identified a good job, you should aggressively explore your transportation options with family and friends. You should ask family and friends if you could car pool with them if the job is near their place of work. If this is not an option, you should ask them if they have any suggestions on ways that you can get to and from work. The key is to explore every possible way that friends or family can help you get to and from work.

---

2. Public Transportation Options

If your family and friends cannot help you get to and from work, then you should explore your public transportation options. You should find out if there is a bus or subway within walking distance from your home that can take you to work and get you home. If there is no public transportation in walking distance from your home, you should ask your family and friends if they will drop you off and pick you up at a public transportation venue that will get you to and from work on time.

3. Reliability of Transportation Options

Once you have identified a family member who will take you to and from work or you have found public transportation that meets your needs, you will have to determine the reliability of that option. Sometimes the transportation provided by family and friends is great at the start of a job. However, they may get tired of dropping you off and picking you up every day and decide not to help you out anymore. In addition, the public transportation options sometimes change. A bus route may change or a subway station is closed. You should prepare for these potential problems by having backup transportation plans. If you are relying on friends or family, then find a backup public transportation route. If you are relying on public transportation, find an alternate public transportation route or identify friends and family that could drop you off at work in case of an emergency.

4. Jobs That Are Reachable Through Available Transportation

Unfortunately, most students do not think about transportation options when searching for a job. They think about the pay, responsibilities, and environment of the job and assume that they will figure out a way to get there if they get the job. There is no excuse for being late to work or missing work because of transportation problems. You must therefore do thorough research about your transportation options before you begin your job search. Once you know what work locations are accessible, you should pursue job opportunities only in these areas. You should do thorough Internet research and talk to as many people as possible about positions in these areas.

5. Jobs That Provide Transportation

There are some jobs that provide transportation. Some companies have vans that pick workers up at certain locations in the morning and drop them off at the same locations after work. Some hospitals, factories, and government locations provide these special vans to increase their employment pool. In addition, some shopping malls pay for these vans because they are interested in hiring students who may not be able to get to and from work otherwise. Jobs that provide transportation are hard to find. However, by searching the Internet and speaking with a lot of different people, you may be able to find a job that provides transportation to and from work.

RECOMMENDATION

There are many obstacles preventing students from finding and succeeding at a job. Transportation is one of the biggest obstacles for students. The students who are willing to do thorough job and transportation research are the ones who are most likely to succeed. The questionnaire on the next page should help you think strategically about exploring your transportation options.

TRANSPORTATION QUESTIONNAIRE

This questionnaire should inspire you to comprehensively research your transportation options. Please answer the transportation questions below by circling either *Yes* or *No*.

1. Do you understand the importance of never being late to work? **Yes No**

2. Can you drive yourself to work every day? **Yes No**

3. Do you have realistic, reliable transportation from a family member? **Yes No**

4. Do you have realistic, reliable transportation from a friend? **Yes No**

5. Is there public transportation to work within walking distance from your home? **Yes No**

6. Do you have friends or family members who can drive you to a location that has public transportation to your place of work? **Yes No**

7. Are all of your transportation options reliable? **Yes No**

8. Are you only looking for jobs that you can get to on time every day? **Yes No**

9. Are you looking for job opportunities that provide transportation? **Yes No**

10. Will you try to arrive at work early every day? **Yes No**

This TRANSPORTATION QUESTIONNAIRE will help you determine how you will get to work. You should explore in greater detail the transportation options available to you. This additional research will help you choose a job location that is easy for you to reach early every day.

CHAPTER 13

Why Is It Important To Be Mentally and Physically Healthy?

Mental and Physical Health

Most good jobs are demanding. They require workers to be passionate, smart, and energetic. Successful employees must have the ability to be self-motivated and work with many different types of people. They must be able to analyze problems and develop effective solutions to the work challenges that they face. They must also have the energy and stamina necessary to complete difficult and time-consuming tasks. In other words, to succeed at work you must be mentally and physically healthy.

All too often people assume that individuals who are considered mentally healthy are academically successful. They believe that the only real measure of one's mental capabilities is how they perform on tests of intellect. However, there are two very different types of intelligence guided by different parts of the brain. The *neocortex* controls the "rational thought" generated by the brain. This part of the brain plays a critical role in determining how you process and analyze information. The *amygdala* controls the "emotional thought" generated by the brain. This part of the brain plays a critical role in determining what your emotional response is to different situations.

Your success at work depends both on rational thought (how you analyze problems) and emotional thought (how you manage your feelings). To be mentally healthy, you must therefore be emotionally and rationally (or intellectually) intelligent. To be physically healthy, your body must be in good shape both internally and externally. Consequently, to succeed at work, you must be healthy in the following three ways:

1. Emotionally
2. Rationally
3. Physically

We describe each of these very different aspects of health below.

---

1. Emotional Health

Unfortunately, few people fully understand how important emotional health is to success at work and life. Many people assume that only smart people are successful. However, the truth is that academic excellence does not guarantee success at work or life. Interestingly, some experts believe that emotional intelligence is more important to success in life and work than rational intelligence. They believe that the way you respond emotionally to problems in life and how you interact with other people is more important than what you know and how well you analyze problems. Both emotional health and rational health are extremely important to success at work and life. There are five key steps to enhancing your emotional health. These are as follows:

a) Personal emotional awareness
b) Emotional self-control
c) Emotional sensitivity
d) Emotional leadership
e) Setting emotional health goals

a) Personal Emotional Awareness

The first step in becoming emotionally healthy is to understand your personal emotional needs. It is extremely important for you to know what stimulates your emotions the most. You should also understand what your emotional strengths and limitations are. In addition, you should

136

attempt to examine your feelings of self-worth and belonging. This is often extremely difficult for students because it requires a great deal of introspection. Many students have never taken time to examine their true feelings. They go through life dealing with challenges as they come along instead of reflecting on who they are and what stimulates them emotionally. The best way to begin to take this emotional inventory is to write down and reflect on the answers to the following three questions:

1) What ten things make me the happiest emotionally?
2) What ten things make me the saddest emotionally?
3) What other things in my life stimulate me emotionally?

Clearly, developing a thorough understanding of your emotional self is a complicated task. However, it is extremely important for you to become aware of the role that emotion plays in your life. Whether you know it or not, you are exposed to emotional stimulants almost every day. Television commercials are designed to stimulate you emotionally to convince you to think about buying a product. Movies utilize different music and visuals to stimulate emotions such as laughter, fear, or sadness. Classmates and co-workers will do things to attempt to stimulate your emotions. By understanding your emotional preferences and stimulants you will have a better sense of how to motivate yourself to achieve maximum success at work and in life.

b) Emotional Self-Control

The second step in becoming emotionally healthy is to learn how to effectively manage your emotions. Once you have developed a good understanding of your emotional stimulants you are ready to begin to enhance your ability to manage your emotions. There are five keys to managing your emotions. These are:

1) Keep unproductive emotions in check.
2) Accept responsibility for your emotional state.
3) Adjust your emotional response to certain situations.
4) Focus on achieving a goal.
5) Do not lose your optimism.

Keep Unproductive Emotions in Check

One of the most difficult things for students to do is control their emotions. Many students have friends that publicly display how they feel and encourage others to do the same. These individuals often do not think about the consequences of this emotional display. Frequently, they hurt others emotionally or even physically. You must learn to manage your emotions at work. You may be angry, frustrated, or bored in your job. However, if you want to keep the job, you must learn how to develop emotional self-control. For example, if you have a short temper, you should acknowledge this and practice counting to ten before reacting in anger.

Accept Responsibility for Your Emotional State

Most people have a tendency to blame others for their feelings. It is critical that you take responsibility for both your positive and negative emotional states.

Adjust Your Emotional Response to Certain Situations

You should know yourself well enough to adjust your emotional reactions to situations in a way that will allow you to effectively respond to these situations. For example, if you get angry when someone criticizes you, you should anticipate that criticism and manage your emotions so that you do not respond angrily to someone's comments.

Focus on Achieving a Goal

One of the best ways to manage your emotions is to focus on a specific goal that forces you to ignore negative emotions that will prevent you from achieving the goal. If a goal is significant to you, it will be easier for you to manage the most difficult emotions to control.

Do Not Lose Your Optimism

Everyone faces some extremely difficult situations both at work and in life. It is very easy to take a negative view of work and life. It is much more difficult to maintain an optimistic viewpoint. You will only be able to effectively manage your emotions if you maintain an optimistic outlook on work and life.

c) Emotional Sensitivity

The third step in becoming emotionally healthy is to learn how to understand other people's emotional needs. Once you understand how to identify and manage your personal emotional needs, you are ready to understand the emotional needs of others. One of the major secrets of individuals who are successful at work and in life is their ability to interact easily with other people. They are effective with people because they have a keen sensitivity to the emotional needs of others. People therefore want to spend time with them because of their unique sensitivity to emotional needs. You should therefore make every effort to develop the ability to understand other people's emotional needs. There are five keys to understanding the emotional needs of others. These are:

1) Take time to observe the emotional responses of people you know well.
2) Take time to observe the emotional responses of people who you don't know well.
3) Anticipate how people will react.
4) Understand emotional office politics.
5) Understand the emotional needs of a group.

Take Time to Observe the Emotional Responses
of People You Know Well

Most people are so focused on themselves that they do not take the time to understand how other people feel. You should observe how friends and family behave in certain situations and make a mental note of their emotional responses. This will be very difficult at first. However, the more you do it, the better you will be at understanding the emotional stimulants of others.

Take Time to Observe the Emotional Responses of People Who You Don't Know Well

Once you have successfully observed the emotional responses of people that you know, you are ready to do the same with people who you do not know well. Observe how co-workers behave in certain work situations and make a mental note of their emotional responses. For example, if you have a boss that gets angry often, understand what makes him angry and why he overreacts emotionally.

Anticipate How People Will React

Once you are able to effectively observe and record individual emotional responses, you should attempt to anticipate emotional responses. You should observe the emotional interactions of other people and guess what each person's emotional response will be. Eventually, you will learn to anticipate how people react emotionally to certain situations.

Understand Emotional Office Politics

One of the most difficult things to do at work is to understand the emotional politics of an office. In some offices, there are people who have "checked out" emotionally while others manipulate the emotions of co-workers. You should make every effort to understand this emotional office politics, so that you can be ready for any emotional stress that you may experience because of the dynamics of the office.

Understand the Emotional Needs of a Group

Every cohesive group develops collective emotional responses to certain situations. Both sports teams and offices develop a personality with a complex inventory of situation-based emotional responses. This personality determines why some offices are very successful and some sports teams win championships. It is extremely difficult to understand the emotional personality of a group. However, to prepare you for future leadership positions, you should attempt to begin to understand group emotions. The most effective senior executives and coaches understand a group's emotional needs.

d) Emotional Leadership

The fourth step in becoming emotionally healthy is to learn how to help people meet their emotional needs. Once you have learned to manage your own emotions and have developed a sensitivity to the emotional needs of others, you are ready to become an "Emotional Leader." An emotional leader is not an executive that cries all of the time. An emotional leader is someone who stimulates the positive emotions in others to achieve a common goal. Most people, whether they admit it or not, are looking for someone to lead them. They are interested in following someone who understands their emotional needs and can help them meet these needs. Successful leaders in business, politics, or sports know that in order to be effective, they must become emotional leaders who can help their followers meet specific emotional needs. If you want to reach the highest level of success in a career or life, you must become an emotional leader. There are five key steps to becoming an emotional leader. These are:

1) Become an effective listener and observer.
2) Partner with others to achieve common objectives.
3) Be recognized as a skilled negotiator.
4) Understand the emotional power of helping others.
5) Develop, guide, and inspire co-workers.

Become an Effective Listener and Observer

Most people do not take time to really listen or observe other people. They are focused on the superficial aspects of a conversation. Emotional leaders not only listen carefully to what other people are saying, they attempt to determine "why they are saying it." They also observe "how they are saying it" to get clues as to "why they are saying it."

For example, a co-worker may say, "Stay away from Joe Smith. He is hard to work with." On a superficial level, it seems that this co-worker is trying to make your life easier by encouraging you to avoid working with Joe Smith. However, this co-worker may really be saying this because he is scared that you may impress Joe Smith and get a promotion that this co-worker wants. You should therefore observe how this co-worker interacts with Joe Smith. If he gets along well with Joe Smith, that is a clue that this person had ulterior motives. You may discover that this person had an emotional need to keep you away from Joe Smith. By listening and observing people in the office, you will become an emotional leader and increase your chances of success.

Partner with Others To Achieve Common Objectives

Emotional leaders understand the emotional needs and desires of others. They therefore become adept at working with diverse groups of people. You should make every effort to partner with your co-workers wherever possible to achieve common objectives. The more you learn to partner with other people, the better you will become at meeting others' emotional needs and succeeding at work.

Be Recognized as a Skilled Negotiator

Conflict resolution is one of the most valuable skills at work. Disagreements, misunderstandings, and bad feelings are very common in offices where people work together for long hours in tight spaces. You should use your ability to understand other people's emotions to resolve these office conflicts and become a hero to your co-workers. Resolving these types of problems is one of the best indicators of successful emotional leadership in a workplace.

Understand the Emotional Power of Helping Others

Helping someone else is a powerful emotional activity that is undervalued by most people. Few people understand that the person helping someone else usually benefits more than the person being helped. By helping others, you are meeting an emotional need to feel important, appreciated, supportive, and successful. If you ever feel sad or disappointed, the best remedy for these bad feelings is to go out and help someone else. This may seem counter-intuitive. However, helping others is one of the best ways to enhance your self-esteem. Experienced emotional leaders understand this and help their co-workers help other people. This type of support in the workplace will increase your visibility and success.

Develop, Guide, and Inspire Co-workers

Successful emotional leaders support the professional and personal development of their co-workers so that they are capable of both meeting their emotional needs and achieving their goals at work. They will guide and inspire their co-workers to meet these goals. You should therefore strive to demonstrate this type of emotional leadership at work. By understanding your own emotional stimulants and being sensitive to others people's emotional stimulants, you can provide emotional leadership and support not only to your co-workers, but to your boss as well. If you can learn to do this, you will be extremely successful no matter where you work or what you do.

e) Setting Emotional Health Goals

The final step in becoming emotionally healthy is to learn how to set emotional health goals. Unfortunately, most students do not understand the importance of setting goals. The only way to improve is to identify and achieve concrete goals (which can be defined as measurable objectives in a specified timeframe). A common misconception about goal setting is that its only benefit is achieving the targeted goal. However, the real benefit of goal setting is the learning that takes place while you are in pursuit of a goal. By setting emotional goals, you will learn about managing your own emotions and becoming an emotional leader. The best way to become emotionally healthy is to practice Emotional Skills Management© (ESM) which is founded on the belief that you must develop the skill to inspire positive emotions in yourself and others. You can do this in as little as four months by setting one ESM goal a month for four months.

Your first ESM goal should be to observe your emotional state for a month. Write down the situations where you laughed, cried, got angry, and were bored. You should keep everything that you write down confidential, if possible, so that no one will be offended by what you put on paper. Obviously, you cannot write down every situation. However, by setting a goal to observe your emotions for a month, you will learn a lot about what stimulates you emotionally.

Once you have achieved this goal, your second ESM goal should be to practice managing your emotions for a month. When you are angry, you should count to 10 before responding. When you are feeling sad, you should do something that makes you happy. You should write down how you felt and what you did to manage those emotions. This exercise will help you begin to learn to manage your emotions.

Your third ESM goal should be to observe the emotions of friends, family, and co-workers for a month and write down what stimulates them emotionally. This will give you a deeper insight into who these people are and what is important to them.

Your final ESM goal should be to positively stimulate the emotions of friends and family. Once you have recorded the emotional stimulants of your friends, family, and co-workers, you should begin to develop a strategy to inspire them emotionally. When someone is sad, you should do something that makes that person happy. When someone is angry, you should attempt to make the person laugh. The more you practice positively stimulating other people's emotions, the more successful you will be interacting with other people. If you follow this four-month ESM program, there is a good chance that you will enhance your success in work and life because you will be a more valued friend and co-worker because of your enhanced emotional health.

2. Rational Health

The term "Rational Health" is rarely used because most people do not understand that mental health is comprised of both emotional health and rational health. The term "intellectual" is used more often than "rational" in the context of mental health. Therefore, the terms "rational" and "intellectual" will be used interchangeably. It is extremely important that you understand the interrelationship of emotional and rational health as you attempt to enhance your mental health for success in work and life.

Society clearly values the intellectual capability of people. People like Albert Einstein have become legends because of their skills in rational thinking. Students who do well in school are given greater respect than students who struggle in school. Unfortunately, society categorizes people unfairly. Some people are assumed to be smart while others are not. However, what most people do not know is that your intellectual capabilities can be enhanced in much the same way that you can get in shape physically.

The phrase "no pain, no gain" applies to both intellectual and physical health. To get healthy physically, you must push your body by exercising regularly. Likewise, to increase your intellectual capabilities, you must push yourself intellectually. If you continually challenge yourself intellectually, you can improve your communication skills, analytical skills, and memory. You will therefore be more successful at work and life because of your enhanced intellectual capabilities. Whether you are a good student or a struggling student, you have the capacity to be healthy intellectually. There are five key steps to enhancing your intellectual health. These steps are the following:

- a) **Maximize your knowledge.**
- b) **Enhance your analytical skill.**
- c) **Refine your verbal communication skills.**
- d) **Use your intelligence.**
- e) **Set rational health goals.**

Maximize Your Knowledge

The easiest way to enhance your intellectual health is to try to learn as much as you can about relevant subjects. The Internet provides an almost infinite amount of information on virtually every subject. You should identify the subjects that are of interest and learn as much as you can about them. For example, if you want to be a doctor, you should do as much research as you can about the profession, the human body, and common illnesses. You should not wait until you get to medical school to research this information. You should do as much research as you can as soon as possible so that you will be ready if you are presented with opportunities to learn more about medicine. By doing this kind of research on an important subject of interest, you will be taking the first step in achieving intellectual health.

Enhance Your Analytical Skills

The ability to solve problems is an essential skill for intellectual health and success in work and life. We are all faced with problems every day. We may have a difficult assignment at school or problematic challenges at work and home. If you are able to effectively analyze your problems, you will be able to develop a solution to them. Individuals who are effective at solving problems are able to achieve their goals at work and in life. The key to effective analysis is the ability to identify the root cause of the problem and break the root cause into its component parts. Typically, each of these parts can be solved in a way that will lead to a solution of the overall problem.

For example, if you are asked to analyze why sales of a product dropped significantly in a month at a clothing store, you are faced with a challenging work problem. The best way to begin to solve the problem is to identify the root cause(s) of the problem. One of the root causes may be that there were several snowstorms during the month that prevented people from getting to the store. Another cause may be that one of the store's competitors had the same item on sale for 20% less. Another cause may be that the item had sold out of its most popular color. Once you identify the root causes of the problem, you can develop solutions to them. You can tell your boss that weather will not be a problem because spring is near, that the price of the item needs to be dropped by 25% to undercut the competitor (if an adequate profit margin still exists), and that the store should buy more of the most popular color of the item. The more you practice this kind of analysis, the better you will be at analyzing and solving problems.

Refine Your Verbal Communication Skills

Unfortunately, people judge your intelligence largely by your ability to communicate. You may be a straight "A" student. However, if you are not able to effectively convey your thoughts verbally, people may not consider you to be as smart as you are. People make these rash judgments based on your communication skills because this is the only factor they have to evaluate your intelligence. They will not see your academic transcript or your analysis of world problems. Instead, all they see and hear is what you say and how you speak. You should therefore make every effort to enhance your verbal communication skills to manage how other people view you and enhance your intellectual health.

Use Your Intelligence

To be successful at work, it is important to be smart. However, it is even more important to use your intelligence. Many very smart students do not do well at work because they are scared to use their intelligence. They are intimidated by their co-workers and are afraid to speak up. They lack confidence in their intellect and are scared that they will say something wrong. You should make every effort to let your boss and co-workers know how smart you are. Because you will likely be the youngest person in the office, there is less risk in speaking up. People do not expect you to know as much as people who have worked in the organization for many years. Consequently, if you do say something that demonstrates your intelligence, they will think that you are brilliant because they did not expect you to be so smart.

Set Rational Health Goals

The final step in becoming rationally healthy is to learn how to set rational health goals. As mentioned in the section on emotional health, the only way to improve your health is to identify and achieve concrete goals. By setting rational health goals, you will learn how to enhance your intellectual capabilities and become rationally healthy. You should practice Rational Skills Management© (RSM) which is founded on the belief that the best way to enhance your rational health is through regular intellectual skills development. You can do this in as little as four months by setting one RSM goal a month for four months.

Your first RSM goal in the first month should be to expand your knowledge. You should begin by attempting to expand your vocabulary. Buy a vocabulary book for standardized tests (or search the Internet for word lists) and memorize as many new words as possible for a month. Your vocabulary plays an important role in your intellectual health and how people perceive you. You should also identify ten important subjects that are important to your career success and research these subjects on the Internet. You may choose to research a particular career or learn about a geographic area or some particular aspect of history. This research exercise will not only increase your knowledge, it will help you identify potential careers. You should focus the first month on enhancing your vocabulary and subject knowledge.

Your second RSM goal should be to focus on enhancing your problem-solving skills in the second month. You should buy a book of word problems (or search the Internet for word problems) and practice solving these problems. At first, solving these problems may seem to be extremely difficult. However, the more you practice, the more comfortable your brain becomes at problem solving. You should also practice writing down any difficult problems that you face in school, at home, or at work. Once you write these problems down, you should write down different possible solutions to each problem. You will find that solving problems is much easier when you write them down. You will also find that the more you practice solving these problems, the better you will become at finding solutions.

Your third RSM goal should be to enhance your verbal and written communication skills in the third month. You should take advantage of the new vocabulary words that you learned in the first month and practice using them in sentences. You should also practice using complete grammatically proper sentences when you speak. You will find that it is often difficult to speak without using slang words. However, you will be more likely to succeed at work if you can demonstrate that you have excellent verbal communication skills. You should also practice enhancing your writing skills. You should begin writing an autobiography to force you to develop the habit of writing regularly. Everyone should write an autobiography because it helps them reflect on their life accomplishments and goods. The autobiography can also give insight into what they should do next in life (with respect to career, relationships, family, etc.). The autobiography does not have to be written for publication. For most people, it will be a confidential personal document of their life. Diaries also help a person develop writing skills. However, frequently, diaries record how the author feels and do not provide any structured information about a person's life that can be useful in helping plan for the future. The more frequently that you write, the more comfortable you become conveying your thoughts in writing.

Your final RSM goal should be to practice using your intelligence. You should make every effort to use your expanded vocabulary and enhanced verbal communication skills at school, work, and home. You should share what you have learned in your Internet research. You should demonstrate (where appropriate) your newly developed problem-solving skills. You should also take every opportunity that you can to demonstrate your enhanced ability to write. The more that you demonstrate these rational health skills, the more successful you will become in work and life.

---

3. Physical Health

There are many books claiming to have the secret of achieving physical health. Some books claim that diet alone will keep you healthy while other books claim that their exercise program is the secret to becoming physically healthy. The real secret to attaining physical health is the same secret to attaining emotional and rational health. The only way to become healthy is plain old hard work. There are no shortcuts to health. To be physically healthy, you should eat a balanced diet every day, exercise regularly, and ensure that your body and blood are healthy. There are five key steps to enhancing your physical health. These steps are as follows:

a) **Eat properly.**
b) **Exercise regularly.**
c) **Maximize your blood health.**
d) **Look healthy.**
e) **Set physical health goals.**

Eat Properly

Most people eat at least three meals a day. Since eating is one of the most frequent health-related activities, your diet will have more impact on your health than anything else. If you eat balanced meals, then you will be extremely healthy nutritionally. If you eat unhealthy meals, then you risk poor health because of a nutritional imbalance. You should therefore attempt to eat a meal with a healthy balance of protein, carbohydrates, and fat. In addition, you should determine the total calories of each meal. You should make sure that you are not gaining weight because you are eating more calories than you are burning off. You should check the Internet to get specific information on government recommended nutritional requirements. By eating properly, you will have more energy and stamina to complete your work assignments.

Exercise Regularly

The second most important thing that you can do to improve your physical health is exercise regularly. Eating healthy meals is a great start to becoming healthy physically. However, it is not enough. You must do repetitive activities designed to increase your strength, flexibility, speed and stamina at least three times a week. This regular exercise will help you sleep better, reduce your chances of getting sick, give you more energy, make you feel better and extend your life. Most successful people recognize the value of exercise and take time out of their busy schedule to exercise at least three times a week. You should do the same so that you can improve your chances of success at work and in life.

Maximize Your Blood Health

Blood is the fuel of your body. Healthy blood levels increase your energy and reduce your chance of illness. Unfortunately, most people do not take the time to have their blood tested to determine their blood health. You should ask your physician to determine your blood health. By monitoring your blood health regularly, you will enhance your physical health.

Look Healthy

Unfortunately, perception is often reality. People frequently determine whether or not you are healthy or a good worker based on how you look.

Workers who appear to be in good shape are given more opportunities than those who appear to be out of shape. This is not fair. However, it is a tragic reality of the workplace. You should therefore make a special effort to try to maintain a healthy weight based on a height / weight scale approved by your physician. By maintaining a healthy weight, you will feel better and maximize your opportunities for success at work.

Set Physical Health Goals

The final step in becoming physically healthy is to learn how to set physical health goals. As mentioned in the section on emotional health, the only way to improve your health is to set and achieve concrete goals. By setting physical health goals, you will learn how to enhance your physical capabilities. You should practice Physical Skills Management© (PSM) which is founded on the belief that the best way to become physically healthy is to develop the skills necessary to eat properly, manage your blood health, and increase your strength, flexibility, speed, and endurance. You can do this by setting four PSM goals.

Your first PSM goal should be to develop the skill to eat a nutritionally balanced meal every day and get 7-8 hours of sleep every night. You should make sure that you have a healthy balance of protein, carbohydrates, and fat. You should also count the number of calories you are eating every day. This will not be easy. It is very difficult to break your current eating habits. In addition to eating well, you should force yourself to get 7 to 8 hours of sleep every night. Your body and mind need to have sufficient rest to function at maximum capacity every day. It is a lot of fun to stay up late every night. However, you increase your chances of getting sick when you do not have enough sleep. You will find that if you eat healthy meals and get sufficient sleep, you will have more energy and feel better about life.

Your second PSM goal should be to develop the skill to exercise regularly. You should identify exercises that enhance your strength, flexibility, speed, and endurance. Exercises like weight lifting will help you increase your strength; yoga will help you increase your flexibility; tennis will help you increase your speed; and, running, biking, and/or swimming will help you develop greater endurance. To maximize the benefits from these exercises, you should do them regularly and follow a specific exercise program (ideally approved by your doctor).

You may want to use the Caldwell Running Equivalent© (CRE) system for your exercise goal setting. In the CRE method, you use running 1 mile as the standard and measure every other exercise against that standard. For example, *Running 1 mile = 1 CRE; Biking 4 miles = 1 CRE; Swimming .25 miles = 1 CRE; 20 minutes of Tennis = 1 CRE (this is Singles not Doubles); 30 minutes of Weightlifting = 1 CRE; 30 minutes of Yoga = 1 CRE.* This conversion is not an exact science because the actual conversion depends on the intensity of your exercise. Another method to compare exercises is to estimate the calories burned. However, that method can get extremely complicated and confusing. The CRE method is an easy way to set goals. You may want to set a goal of 7 CREs a week and complete enough exercises every week to accomplish this goal. For example, if you complete 30 minutes of Yoga, 2 miles of Running, 1 hour of Tennis and 30 minutes of Weightlifting, you have achieved your goal of 7 CREs. Likewise, if you Bike 4 miles and play 2 hours of Tennis, you achieve your goal of 7 CREs. The CRE method gives you the flexibility to try different combinations of exercises to achieve your weekly goals.

Your third PSM goal is to make sure that your blood is healthy. Your blood health will play an important role in determining how much energy you have to achieve your goals at work and in life. You should ask your physician to determine the key measures of blood health and test your blood accordingly. Some physicians believe that by measuring your *Total Cholesterol, High-Density Lipoprotein (HDL) Cholesterol, Triglycerides, Glucose, Uric Acid, and Insulin,* you can determine a person's blood health. Other physicians believe that there are other ways to measure blood health. When you receive the test results, you should ask your physician what you need to do to improve your blood health. Once you receive direction from your physician, you should do whatever is necessary to achieve your blood health goals.

The final PSM goal will be the most difficult of all. You should refocus your efforts on the aspect of physical health that is the most challenging. If you find it difficult to eat a nutritional meal every day, then you should force yourself to change your diet. If you do not have the discipline to exercise regularly, then you should adjust your schedule accordingly. If you have trouble doing what is required to enhance your blood health, then you should try again. Most people know what they need to do to be physically healthy. Unfortunately, they are not willing to do what it takes to achieve this goal. Your goals for career and life success should motivate you to push yourself to do whatever is necessary to become physically healthy.

RECOMMENDATION

You should attempt to increase your emotional, rational, and physical health to maximize your enjoyment of work and life. Ideally, you will follow the ESM plan to enhance your emotional health; the RSM plan to enhance your rational health; and the PSM plan to enhance your physical health. If you dedicate yourself to improving your skills in each of these areas, you will be well positioned for incredible success in everything that you do. One of the most effective ways to measure how healthy you are is to complete the EMOTIONAL, RATIONAL, AND PHYSICAL (ERP) SKILLS MANAGEMENT EVALUATION on the next page.

ERP SKILLS MANAGEMENT EVALUATION

It requires a great deal of hard work to maximize your emotional, rational, and physical health. One way to assess how hard you are working to become healthy in these areas is to complete the EMOTIONAL, RATIONAL, AND PHYSICAL (ERP) SKILLS MANAGEMENT EVALUATION below. Please weight each of the statements from 5 to 1 and be as honest as you possibly can:

5 = Always
4 = Almost Always
3 = Frequently
2 = Sometimes
1 = Never

A. ____ I am aware of my personal emotions.

B. ____ I can control my emotions.

C. ____ I am sensitive to other people's emotions.

D. ____ I can inspire other people emotionally.

E. ____ I set emotional health goals.

F. ____ I attempt to maximize my knowledge.

G. ____ I attempt to maximize my analytical skills.

H. ____ I try to refine my communication skills.

I. ____ I try to use my intelligence wherever possible.

J. ____ I set rational health goals.

K. ____ I eat properly.

L. ____ I exercise intensely.

M. ____ I try to improve my blood health.

N. ____ I try to look healthy.

O. ____ I set physical health goals.

By completing this weighting, you will have a much better idea of the areas that you need to improve to achieve emotional, rational, and physical health. You should work very hard to improve those areas where you score a 3 or less.

CHAPTER 14

How Do I Get Promoted?

How To Get Promoted

Now that you have learned to manage your time, improved your ethical sensitivity, started dressing for success, and demonstrated a commitment to mental and physical health, you should focus on getting promoted. There are many incredible benefits of getting promoted. These include higher pay, more responsibility, the opportunity to work on more interesting projects, and greater control of your schedule. Unfortunately, there are many variables that determine your chances of being promoted. You can control some of these variables (like your work performance and work ethic). However, there are many variables that you cannot control (like the attitude of your boss and the number of available promotion opportunities). There is nothing that you can do to guarantee that you will get a promotion. However, your objective should be to increase the probability of getting promoted. There are ten things you should do to increase the chances of being promoted:

1. Understand the company and your responsibilities.
2. Find out what it will take to get promoted.
3. Come to work early every day.
4. Stay late every evening.
5. Manage expectations.
6. Anticipate the needs of your boss.
7. Help other workers do their job.
8. Work on assignments others don't want.
9. Work with a mentor.
10. Find a sponsor.

1. Understand the Company and Your Responsibilities

Before you begin your job, you should develop a good understanding of the company's mission and objectives and your job responsibilities. However, if you want to get promoted, you should intensify your research on the company. You should do a thorough company search on the Internet and look for information that will give you a deeper understanding of the organization and your role in the company. This information will be valuable as you attempt to impress your boss and co-workers. You never know when the information you have pulled off of the Internet will help to complete an important project.

2. Find Out What It Will Take To Get Promoted

Once you have held your job for a few weeks and demonstrated that you are an excellent worker, you should ask your boss, "What do I need to do to be considered for a promotion sometime in the future?" Most bosses will be impressed by this question because it demonstrates that you have a commitment to the job and the company. Hopefully, the boss will provide you with some specific things that you have to accomplish before you can be considered for a promotion. This will give you a good idea of the things you need to do to get promoted. However, not every boss is the same. Some bosses might be offended by the question because they may think that you are trying to get promoted too quickly. You should therefore assess whether or not your boss will be impressed by this question.

3. Come To Work Early Every Day

It is essential for you to come to work early every day. It does not benefit you to come to work early occasionally. Consistency is extremely important in developing a positive impression at work. Arriving early every day demonstrates that you have a commitment to the job and a passion for your work. It also allows you to get a head start on your work assignments so that you can complete them before the assigned deadline. By arriving at work early, it may also give you more time to enhance your relationship with your boss. This can potentially be a big help when promotions are being considered.

4. Stay Late Every Evening

You should also stay late every evening. Staying late every evening has many of the same benefits as arriving early. However, if you do both, you will really impress your boss and probably your boss's boss. Staying late shows a true commitment to the job. In addition, it will provide you with additional opportunities to complete your work and speak to your boss. It also often leads to opportunities to go out to dinner with senior executives in the organization. This exposure can exponentially increase your chances of promotion.

5. Manage Expectations

Managing the expectations of your boss and the other people you work with is one of the major secrets of success at work. If you exceed the expectations of everyone you work with, you will be considered an extremely valuable employee. It is very difficult to exceed expectations without managing them. You should always make promises that you can keep. For example, if you promise your boss you will complete a project on Friday, you should get it to him or her by Thursday. This is considered managing expectations because you are setting an agreed upon deadline that you know that you can exceed. If you consistently manage expectations and turn projects in early, you will develop a reputation as a top worker.

6. Anticipate the Needs of Your Boss

Managers dream of employees who can anticipate their requests. Most managers are so busy doing their job that they often don't have time to tell their employees everything that needs to be done. They look for employees who can identify what needs to be done in advance and do it without receiving direction. Managers will do anything (like give a raise or promotion) to keep these types of employees because they are hard to find. You should observe your boss very closely and become adept at anticipating his or her needs. This will significantly increase your chances for a raise or a promotion.

7. Help Others Do Their Job

Most workplaces encourage teamwork. If one member of the team is having trouble, then the other team members should help out as much as they can. You should make every effort to become a good team player and help your co-workers. You will endear yourself to them and increase the likelihood that they will be supportive of your promotion. In addition, you never know when you will need their help. All too often workers "burn bridges" with co-workers and find themselves stuck when they need help. Make sure that you are considered the best team player in the office.

8. Work on Assignments That Others Don't Want

You should develop a reputation as someone who is willing to work on any project that is available. Many employees only want to work on the best projects. Unfortunately, this limits their chances of promotion because they develop a reputation as "cherry pickers" (people who pick the best or easiest projects). Most organizations want workers who are willing to do whatever is necessary to help the organization. Frequently, the employee who initially volunteers for the unpopular work assignments develops a reputation as a star and never has to work on these projects again. Likewise, the workers who avoid these assignments often are considered average employees and are forced to work on these types of assignments. Always think about the long-term implications of what you do at work. Often, suffering early in your career leads to opportunity later in your career.

9. Work with a Mentor

Mentors are individuals who provide career and life guidance to less experienced individuals. If possible, you should find a mentor in the organization who can help you succeed in the position. This person can tell you who the best people in the company are to work with. They can also tell you what projects to work on to maximize your performance. Mentors are especially valuable to those employees who do not have a lot of work experience. The rules of work are very complicated. Consequently, it can be extremely helpful to have an internal advisor who can help you succeed at work. It can also be helpful to have a mentor who does not work at the company. They can provide an external perspective on your job and life outside of work that would not be provided by an internal mentor. It can be difficult to find a mentor when you are new to an organization. The best way to find a mentor is to speak with your fellow co-workers or friends to get their thoughts about potential mentors in the organization or in the community.

10. Find a Sponsor

Frequently, people confuse mentors with sponsors. Mentors are usually advisors that do not have direct influence on your career. Sponsors are individuals who play a critical role in determining whether you are promoted or if you will get a raise. Typically, a sponsor is your boss or your supervisor's boss. A person will only sponsor you if you play a valuable role in making them successful. For example, if you were on your boss's project team and played a critical role in making the project a success, then your boss will become a sponsor. They will want to keep you on their team so that you can continue to help them succeed. They will also want to keep you happy so that you will stay on their team. As a result, they will do what they can to ensure that you get a raise and/or a promotion.

RECOMMENDATION

There are many tricks to positioning yourself for a promotion at work. You should consciously make a special effort to come to work early, stay late, manage expectations, anticipate your boss's needs, and find a sponsor. By doing these things and more, you will probably be considered a top performer and a leading candidate for promotion. The following PROMOTION QUESTIONNAIRE should help you increase your chances of being promoted.

PROMOTION QUESTIONNAIRE

This questionnaire should inspire you to focus on the ten things you should do to get promoted. Please answer the promotion questions below by circling either *Yes* or *No*.

1. Do you understand the company's mission and objectives and your job responsibilities? **Yes   No**

2. Have you found out what you have to do to get promoted? **Yes   No**

3. Do you come to work early every day? **Yes   No**

4. Do you stay late at work every evening? **Yes   No**

5. Do you manage the expectations of the people who you work with? **Yes   No**

6. Do you anticipate the needs of your boss? **Yes   No**

7. Do you help your co-workers do their job? **Yes   No**

8. Do you volunteer to work on projects that other workers don't want? **Yes   No**

9. Have you found a mentor? **Yes   No**

10. Have you found a sponsor? **Yes   No**

This PROMOTION QUESTIONNAIRE should force you to reflect on the things that you are doing to get promoted. If you answered "Yes" to each of these questions, then you are doing what you can to get promoted. However, if you answered "No" to one or more of these questions, you should make a special effort to do those promotion-related things that you are not doing. You should continue to work on these things until you can accurately answer "Yes" to every question. This exercise will significantly increase the probability that you will be promoted.

CHAPTER 15

What Are the Ten Rules of Career Management?

The Ten Rules of Career Management

Once you have successfully found a job, earned a promotion, and focused on a career, you are ready to think about career management. Getting promoted in a job is very different than career management. A promotion indicates that you can succeed in a job. Career management is a plan to achieve as much as you can throughout many jobs in a career. Unfortunately, most people wait until they are firmly established in their career before seriously thinking about career management. You should begin thinking about career management as soon as you decide what career you are going to pursue. The Ten Rules of Career Management are:

1. Clearly define your career goals.
2. Believe you can succeed.
3. Understand that first impressions are lasting.
4. Know that your reputation is your most valuable asset.
5. Exceed everyone's expectations.
6. Understand that success depends more on attitude than ability.
7. Work harder than everyone else.
8. Find as many sponsors as possible.
9. Be an emotional leader.
10. Remember that you control your destiny.

1. Clearly Define Your Career Goals

Once you have identified your career focus, you should start the process of developing career specific goals. You should begin by identifying your ultimate career goal. Think about the highest level you want to reach in the career of your choice. If you are interested in business, you may want to be president of a large company. If you are interested in becoming a lawyer, then you may want to become a judge. If you want to work for a large nonprofit organization, you may want to become the executive director. You should then list the career positions that you hope to hold before attaining your ultimate career objective. Once you have listed each of these positions, you should list the anticipated timeframes for attaining each position.

2. Believe You Can Succeed

All too often, the only career and life barriers that people really face are those that they place on themselves. People often fail because they do not believe that they can succeed. They are not willing to put forth the necessary effort because (either consciously or subconsciously) they think that they will fail. No matter what your background is, you should believe that you can succeed. If you believe in yourself, you will work as hard as you can to achieve your career or life goals. People in virtually every career and life situation have been able to defy probability and succeed simply because of a strong belief that they will succeed. You must believe in yourself enough to overcome any barriers that you will face in your career.

3. Understand That First Impressions Are Lasting

No matter what career you decide to pursue, you will interact with a lot of different people. One of the secret skills of successful people is the ability to make a positive impression on everyone whom they meet. Unfortunately, first impressions are lasting. If you do not present yourself in a very positive way in an initial meeting with someone, you will likely not get career support from that person. However, a good first impression may lead to a great deal of career support.

In addition, your performance on your first project at a job will impact your success at work. If you do an outstanding job on that first project, you will be viewed as a great employee and will be given increasingly important projects. However, if you do not do well on that first project, you may be labeled as an average or below average worker. Once you have been labeled, it is hard to change how you are viewed. Consequently, you must do everything that you can to make a good first impression both when you meet people and on your first project at work.

4. Know That Your Reputation Is Your Most Valuable Asset

Unfortunately, most people do not understand that having an impeccable reputation is the key to long-term success in work and life. Having a great reputation will help you get a raise and a promotion. It will also increase your ability to attract friends. Having a bad reputation can get you fired, limit your employment opportunities and lead to the loss of friends. You develop a good reputation by being ethical, honest, fair, hardworking and friendly. It is very hard to develop a good reputation. You have to demonstrate these character traits to many people for many years. However, you can lose this positive reputation by doing just one unethical thing. It is therefore extremely important that you do everything that you can to develop a great reputation.

5. Exceed Everyone's Expectations

People are most impressed by individuals who do more than expected. They have certain expectations that people will accomplish or do certain things. The most successful people are those who exceed the expectations of others. They go above and beyond what most people would do in most circumstances. They exceed the expectations of their boss by completing projects early. They exceed the expectations of their co-workers by helping them complete their work. You should therefore focus on exceeding the expectations of everyone that you interact with every day.

6. *Understand That Success Depends More on Attitude Than Ability*

Many of the most talented workers do not succeed because they have a bad attitude. They do a good job on their work assignments; however, they may complain frequently, demonstrate arrogance, or have difficulty working with other people. They therefore do not get promoted and frequently get fired because of this negative attitude. You should maintain a positive attitude at all times. There is never a reason to have a negative attitude. Negativity reduces your ability to solve problems because it stifles creativity. By facing every problem with optimism, you will be able to effectively address problems utilizing analytically-based creative solutions that are stimulated by your positivity.

7. *Work Harder Than Everyone Else*

One of the most obvious keys to success at work is working harder than everybody else. People who work harder are able to complete their assignments at work faster than other employees. They come to work earlier and stay later than others. They earn the respect of their boss and are frequently invited to spend quality time with senior executives in the organization before and after work. They are therefore more likely to get a promotion or a raise. Consequently, to maximize your chances of success in your career, you should attempt to work harder than anyone else in your workplace.

8. *Find as Many Sponsors as Possible*

It is essential that you identify people who are decision makers in your organization who will advocate for a raise or promotion for you. These sponsors will help you succeed at work. No one is ever promoted or given a raise without at least one sponsor. Some individual or group has to review your performance and determine if you deserve to earn more money or gain more responsibility. Your sponsor will be the person who makes your case. He or she will tell stories of how well you did on a project. Your sponsor might let people know that you come to work early and leave late. They might say that you work well with your co-workers. If you can find a sponsor who will make these kinds of statements around evaluation time, you will have a good chance of advancing rapidly in your chosen career. You should therefore do everything that you can to convince one or more sponsors to let other decision makers know how good an employee you are. The more sponsors you have, the more likely you will be to succeed in the career of your choice.

9. Be an Emotional Leader

At some point in your career, you will very likely have an opportunity to assume a leadership position. You may have a chance to manage and lead other people. To many people, the opportunity to lead is frightening. They do not feel that they are ready to take responsibility for the work of other people. Others are excited about the opportunity to build a cohesive team and inspire co-workers. The individuals who look forward to leadership opportunities are typically the most successful managers. They recognize that assuming a managerial position provides a great opportunity for career growth. If you are fortunate enough to hold a managerial position, you should attempt to be an emotional leader.

As an emotional leader, you should not only listen carefully to what people are saying, you should take time to understand what stimulates them emotionally. You should become adept at conflict resolution and support the development of the members of your team. Finally, you should be able to inspire co-workers to accomplish more than they thought was possible. If you are successful at becoming an emotional leader, you will be extremely successful in any career that you choose.

10. Remember That You Control Your Destiny

It is very easy to blame other people for your failures. Excuses like "I have a bad boss" or "my co-workers sabotage my work" are not acceptable reasons for not doing your job. You can still be successful at work even if you have a bad boss or saboteurs as co-workers. You just have to be proactive and accept the fact that you control your destiny. Other people may help you in your work. However, you are the person who determines whether you are a success or failure.

There are solutions to every challenge that you will face at work. You have to develop the ability to overcome any obstacle that stands in the way of your goals. To do this, you must have a strong belief in your ability to succeed. It is essential that you have the self-confidence to face a difficult challenge head on. If you lack the necessary confidence, the challenges are likely to overwhelm you, thereby ensuring that you fail. You should accept responsibility for your successes and failures and passionately believe in your ability to control your destiny throughout your career.

RECOMMENDATION

Doing well at a job is very different than succeeding in a career. To excel in a particular job, you simply need to impress your boss and co-workers. To have an outstanding career, you must develop a long-term plan, establish a track record of success in multiple jobs, and effectively manage your interaction with many different people over many years. It is therefore extremely important that you know as soon as possible what your career aspirations are. This will give you more time to lay a foundation for career success. By completing the following CAREER MANAGEMENT QUESTIONNAIRE, you will have a better understanding of what you need to do to increase the probability of succeeding in the career of your choice.

CAREER MANAGEMENT QUESTIONNAIRE

This questionnaire should inspire you to focus on the Ten Rules of Career Management. Please answer the career management questions below by circling either *Yes* or *No*.

1. Have you clearly defined your career goals? **Yes No**

2. Do you really believe that you can succeed in your chosen career? **Yes No**

3. Do you do what you can to make a positive first impression? **Yes No**

4. Since your reputation is your most valuable asset, do you work on ensuring that you have a great reputation? **Yes** **No**

5. Do you try to exceed everyone's expectations every day? **Yes** **No**

6. Since success depends more on attitude than ability, do you try to maintain a positive attitude every day? **Yes** **No**

7. Do you work harder than everyone else? **Yes** **No**

8. Have you found as many sponsors as possible? **Yes** **No**

9. Are you an "Emotional Leader"? **Yes** **No**

10. Do you truly believe that you control your destiny? **Yes** **No**

You must have complete faith in your ability to accomplish your career goals. There is little room for doubt in your abilities. Consequently, in addition to setting career goals early in life, you should develop a history of success at work that will convince you that you control your professional destiny. No one can stop you from achieving your professional goals if you truly believe in yourself.

This CAREER MANAGEMENT QUESTIONNAIRE should force you to reflect on the things that you need to be aware of to succeed in your career. If you answered "Yes" to each of these questions, then you are doing what you can to succeed in the career of your choice. However, if you answered "No" to one or more of these questions, you should make a special effort to do those career-related things that you are not doing. You should continue to work on these things until you can accurately answer "Yes" to every question. This exercise should significantly increase both your self-confidence and likelihood of career success.

SECTION III

Finanical
and
Life Planning

CHAPTER 16

How Do I Manage My Money?

Managing Your Money

Once you start receiving a regular paycheck, you should begin to think about managing your money and developing a financial plan. Financial planning is the process of reviewing your financial situation and developing a strategy that will enable you to achieve your financial goals. Most people do not develop a financial plan. They struggle financially because they never develop a strategy to maximize their assets. The relatively few people that do develop a financial plan do so when they are close to retirement. They therefore cannot benefit from the incredible compound interest that they would have earned if they developed a financial plan and started investing their money early in life.

Most students are at the perfect age to begin developing a financial plan. Unfortunately, because they typically don't have a lot of money, they do not see the value of a financial plan. People confuse an investment plan with a financial plan. To implement an investment plan, you need money. To implement a financial plan, you only need the vision to develop a strategy to invest your money once you have it. You don't have to have a lot of money to develop a financial plan. Consequently, everyone who has a job should develop a financial plan. The ten key steps to start the process of writing a financial plan are these:

1. Learn about financial planning.
2. Determine your monthly and annual income.
3. Determine your monthly and annual expenses.
4. Find your latest federal and state tax returns.
5. List the value of your assets.
6. List your total liabilities.
7. Create a personal budget and income statement.
8. Create a personal net worth statement.
9. Write down your financial goals.
10. Understand the Financial Planning Pyramid (FPP).

---

1. Learn About Financial Planning

A financial plan is a strategy to manage your money. It is a document designed to tell you how to spend your money for maximum growth. Your financial plan is based on your income, expenses, assets, liabilities, age, and risk tolerance. The plan will clearly outline your financial goals. It will tell you how to invest your money and protect your assets in a way that will increase your net worth. Before you begin developing your financial plan, you should search the Internet for additional information about financial planning.

---

2. Determine Your Income

The first step in developing a financial plan is documenting your income. You should estimate your monthly and annual income. Add up the amount of money that you receive every month from all income sources (i.e. full-time job, part-time job, special paid projects, etc.). This total monthly income is the foundation of your financial plan. You should multiply this monthly amount by 12 to determine your annual income. Your income represents the maximum amount of money that you have to invest.

---

3. Determine Your Expenses

The second step in developing a financial plan is determining your expenses. Most people have no idea how much money they spend every month. They know how much they pay every month for bills. However, they often forget the impulse purchases that they make every day. To get an accurate record of the amount of money that you spend, you should capture your True Monthly Expenses (TME). To determine your TME, you should compile a list of everything that you pay for every day for a month (no matter how much or how little it costs). On a piece of paper, you should list the date of the purchase, describe the purchase, and list the amount of the purchase. The TME sheet will give you an accurate record of what you are spending each month. For many people, the TME will show that hundreds of dollars a month are wasted on things that they don't need. In many cases, these dollars should be redirected toward investments. Once you have totaled the TME, multiply it by 12 to determine your estimated annual expenses.

---

4. Find Your Latest State and Federal Tax Returns

Most students have never made enough money on their own to file extensive federal and state tax returns. However, even if you have never filed a return, you should take the time to understand how taxes are filed so that you can begin to develop a strategy to minimize your taxes. Individuals who are not dependents of someone else and who generate income are typically required to file federal and state tax returns. The money collected from these taxes pays for most of the operating expenses of the federal, state, and local government. The bad news is that the more money you make, the more taxes you will have to pay. The good news is that there are ways to reduce your taxes.

The goal of tax planning is to legally reduce the amount of money that you pay in taxes. One way to reduce your taxable income is to contribute to a charity. The money contributed to some charities can be legally deducted from your taxable income, thereby reducing your taxes. There are many other ways to reduce your taxes. For your financial plan, you should collect any tax forms that you have filed. If you have not filed taxes yet, you should do an extensive Internet search on federal and state taxes to learn more about this important part of financial planning.

5. List the Value of Your Assets

The next step in developing a financial plan is to total the value of everything that you own. This total represents your assets. Calculating the value of your assets is the first step in determining how much money you are worth (commonly called your "net worth"). You should write down the name and value of your assets on a sheet of paper. The most challenging thing about doing this is determining the market value of each of these items. The market value is the amount that someone would pay today for a particular item. For example, if you paid $500 for a television two years ago, then you should estimate what someone would pay for the television today. You should guess what the resale value of everything you own (i.e. your car, clothes, computers, money in the bank, savings, etc.) would be and list the amount on the sheet. Once you have completed this list and totaled the value of the items, you will know the total value of your assets.

6. List the Value of Your Liabilities

Once you have totaled your assets, you should total the value of everything that you owe. The money that you owe is called a "liability." For example, any student loans, credit cards, car loans, mortgages, etc. are considered liabilities. You should write down, on a piece of paper, the name and total amount of each liability. You should summarize the total of these liabilities at the bottom of the paper. This number represents your total liabilities (or total debt). Once you have recorded your liabilities, you should examine them to determine if there is any way for you to reduce your total liabilities.

Unfortunately, because it is very easy to get approval for credit cards, most people (including many students) are heavily in debt. They therefore have a large part of their income consumed by credit card debt repayment. It is extremely important that you minimize your credit card debt and other liabilities. Many students lack the financial discipline necessary to use credit cards for emergencies. They run up a tremendous amount of debt that ruins their credit and prevents them from getting loans for things like cars and houses in the future. You should not get a credit card until you have graduated from school and have a full-time job.

7. Create a Personal Budget

It is extremely important for you to develop personal financial statements. Financial statements show you how much money you have and what you need to do to be financially healthy. The first step in developing financial statements is to create a budget. There are five steps to creating an effective budget:

a) Learn about budgeting.
b) Write down your total monthly income.
c) Write down your total monthly expenses.
d) Review your income and expenses.
e) Prepare your monthly budgets.

Learn About Budgeting

Understand that budgeting is the key to managing your money and preventing you from spending more than you earn. You should search the Internet for more information about budgeting if you do not feel that you have a full grasp of the concept.

Write Down Your Total Monthly Income

This typically includes your income from work, any income from investments, and any regular financial support that you receive from your family or somewhere else.

Write Down Your Total Monthly Expenses

This information should be based on the TME sheet that you developed earlier.

Review Your Income and Expenses To Ensure That They Are Realistic

Make sure that the income that you list is net of taxes. In addition, make sure that your expenses include everything that you are likely to spend. Once you feel comfortable that you have accurate income and expense numbers for one month, you should estimate what your income and expenses will be for a full year. If your monthly income and expenses will be consistent, then simply multiply your monthly numbers by 12 to get the annual totals. If the monthly numbers will vary, then you should estimate the income and expenses for each of the 12 months.

Prepare Your Monthly Budget

You should first subtract your monthly expenses from your monthly income to determine your net income or loss every month. Next, you should subtract your annual expenses from your annual income to determine your net income or loss for a full year. If you have money left over after this calculation, then you are living within your means. If you are losing money every month or year, then you should do everything you can to reduce your expenses or increase your income so that you have money for savings.

A sample Monthly Budget and Annual Budget for Jane Johnson follows:

Jane Johnson's MONTHLY Budget

INCOME

Monthly Salary (after taxes)	$2,700
Supplemental Income from Second Job or from Family	600
TOTAL INCOME	$3,300

EXPENSES

Food	$ 650
Rent	975
Entertainment/Clothing	150
Student Loan Payments	725
Credit Card Payments	120
Telephone Bill	95
Cable/Internet/Computer-Related Expenses	140
Investments	100
Charitable Donations	25
Miscellaneous (postage, supplies, etc.)	160
TOTAL EXPENSES	$3,140
NET INCOME (or LOSS)	$160

Jane Johnson's ANNUAL Budget

INCOME

Monthly Salary (after taxes)	$32,400
Supplemental Income from Second Job or from Family	7,200
TOTAL INCOME	$39,600

EXPENSES

Food	$ 7,800
Rent	11,700
Entertainment/Clothing	1,800
Student Loan Payments	8,700
Credit Card Payments	1,440
Telephone Bill	1,140
Cable/Internet/Computer-Related Expenses	1,680
Investments	1,200
Charitable Donations	300
Miscellaneous (postage, supplies, etc.)	1,920
TOTAL EXPENSES	$37,680
NET INCOME (or LOSS)	$ 1,920

---

8. Create a Personal Net Worth Statement

Your net worth is the ultimate measure of your financial health. Your net worth represents everything that you own minus everything that you owe. Your net worth statement consists of all of your assets (money in your checking account, investments, computer, television, jewelry, clothes, car, etc.) and all your liabilities (student loans, credit card debt, auto loans, mortgage, etc.). Your net worth is the difference between your assets and liabilities. Your main financial goal should be to maximize your net worth. Unfortunately, many students, because of student loans and credit card debt, have a negative net worth. However, the proper financial and career planning will help you maximize your net worth over the long run.

A sample net worth statement for Jane Johnson follows. As you can see, largely because of student loan debt, Jane Johnson has a negative net worth. Her investment in her education will pay off if she becomes successful in the career of her choice. Her income will enable her to pay off her student loans and make investments necessary to turn her negative net worth into a positive net worth.

Jane Johnson's Net Worth Statement

ASSETS

Checking Account Balance	$ 1,750
Investment Balance	2,375
Car	14,500
Appliances	3,500
Jewelry	5,250
Clothes	1,650
Other Personal Assets	1,100
TOTAL ASSETS	$30,125

LIABILITIES

Credit Card Balances	$ 1,250
Student Loans	27,350
Car Loan	10,760
TOTAL LIABILITIES	$39,360
NET WORTH (Negative)	($ 9,235)

---

9. Write Down Your Financial Goals

The foundation of your financial plan is your financial goals and objectives. You must set your personal financial goals and objectives based on your education, income, career choice, life choices, and long-term net worth objectives. Obviously, if your career choice is one that has not historically made people wealthy, your financial goals would be more modest than those of someone going into a career where most people make a lot of money. Likewise, you may prefer to help other people than make a lot of money so your financial goals should reflect that decision. However, if maximizing your personal net worth is a major financial goal, you must choose a career and lifestyle that will allow you to achieve this goal.

Your financial goals should be divided into three categories. The first relates to your financial objectives. You should answer the question: "What is my personal net worth goal?" The second category relates to your career choice. You should answer the following two important questions: "What is my career choice? Will it support my financial objectives?" The final category relates to life choices. You should answer the following three questions: "What is important to me in life (luxury, travel, helping others, relaxing, etc.)? Does this match my financial objectives? Does this match my career choice?" If the answers to these questions are not consistent in all three of these categories, then you should revise your financial goals and objectives accordingly.

---

10. Understand the Financial Planning Pyramid

The Financial Planning Pyramid (FPP) is a simple visual guide to managing your money. It is also a useful way to analyze your personal financial health. The FPP is provided below:

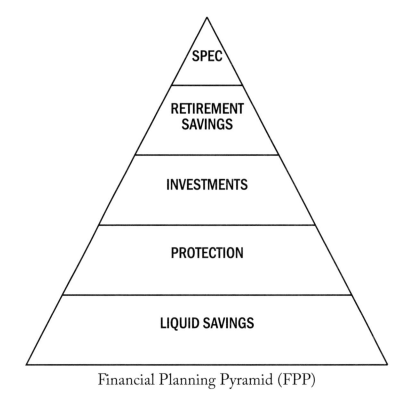

Financial Planning Pyramid (FPP)

The FPP has five different compartments. The base compartment of the FPP is the widest because it is the foundation of your financial plan. The base compartment represents your "Liquid Savings." You should have approximately 3 to 6 months of gross income in a fairly safe investment in the Liquid Savings compartment of the FPP. Savings are considered liquid if you have access to your money within seven days. Liquid savings include checking accounts, money market accounts, certificates of deposit (CDs), and low risk mutual funds. The size of this compartment signifies its importance, not the total dollar amount invested in this category. Typically, once you are investing regularly, you will have more money in investments than in liquid savings. However, you need to have sufficient liquid savings well before you think of investing. If you do not have sufficient liquid savings, you will not have enough money in the event of emergencies.

The second compartment of the FPP is "Protection." This includes automobile, disability, health, homeowners, life, property, and other insurances. Insurance protects against catastrophic problems that you could not afford to pay for otherwise. Without the proper insurance, many people are at risk for bankruptcy.

The third compartment of the FPP is "Investment Savings." Once you have the appropriate liquid savings and protection, you can begin to save for your financial goals through your "Investment Savings." Investment savings can be in the form of mutual funds, conservative stocks, bonds, and annuities.

The fourth compartment is for "Retirement Savings." This compartment is for any money that you have in long-term savings, specifically for retirement. This includes work pension funds or 401-K funds or their equivalent.

The fifth and final compartment is for "Speculation." This is where you list high-risk investments in which you could potentially lose the money that you invested. This includes speculative stocks, precious metals, and commodities. If you are not familiar with these investments, you should research them on the Internet for additional information.

The FPP tells you how to reallocate your money to maximize your financial health. If you do not have six months' gross income in your "Liquid Savings" or have insufficient "Protection" or not enough money in "Investment Savings" or no "Retirement Savings" or too much money in "Speculation" to achieve your financial goals, you need to address these problems.

The Ten Rules of Financial Planning

Completing the ten steps required to prepare for developing a financial plan is in many ways harder than developing the financial plan. If you have successfully completed each of the ten preparation steps, you know how to develop your monthly and annual budget, how to measure your net worth, and how to set financial planning goals. You are now ready to begin to develop a personal financial plan by following ten simple rules. The ten rules of financial planning are these:

1. Create a liquid savings strategy.
2. Create an insurance strategy.
3. Create an investment strategy.
4. Create a retirement strategy.
5. Create a speculation strategy.
6. Develop a personal Financial Planning Pyramid (FPP).
7. Maintain excellent credit.
8. Focus on maximizing your net worth.
9. Begin the process of tax planning.
10. Develop and implement your financial plan.

1. Create a Liquid Savings Strategy

You must start your financial plan by saving sufficient money to ensure that you have enough money for all your expenses and that your monthly bills are paid on time. You must open a checking account as soon as you have money to put into the bank. Unfortunately, many people use check-cashing services, instead of opening a bank account, and pay unnecessary fees for their own money. You should find a bank near your house and open a checking account as soon as possible. This account will allow you to keep your money in a safe place and enable you to pay your bills with checks or debit cards.

Your liquid savings strategy should be focused on ensuring that you have at least one month of gross income in a checking account and three to six times your True Monthly Expenses (TME) in investments that allow you withdraw money within seven days without penalty. The one month of gross income in the checking account will ensure that you pay your bills on time. The additional money will guarantee that you have money in the event of a financial emergency (you lose your job, you need a new car, etc.). The three to six months of TME money can be invested in money market accounts or other safe mutual fund investments.

2. Create an Insurance Strategy

Insurance is one of the most misunderstood investment vehicles. Many people purchase too much insurance or the wrong insurance because of an overly aggressive insurance agent. However, most people do not purchase enough insurance because they do not know the benefits of risk protection. The five major types of insurance are health, life, disability, homeowners, and auto insurance. Insurance is an important part of an investment portfolio because it protects your assets in the case of a catastrophe. You may have a solid financial plan that will help you achieve all of your financial goals; however, illness, disability, death, bad weather, or an auto accident can destroy your solid financial plan. Insurance allows you to protect against these potential life challenges. Here is a brief description about each of the major types of insurance. However, you should do additional research on the Internet to learn more about insurance.

- *Health Insurance*

   Health insurance helps you pay for the cost of medical care. Most people acquire their health insurance through their companies and therefore do not pay the full cost of basic health care (they benefit from group coverage). Unfortunately, the cost of health insurance outside of group coverage is extremely high. However, paying for health insurance is a necessary expense. Without health insurance, a major illness can leave you bankrupt.

- *Life Insurance*

Life insurance protects your dependent (people who rely on you for income) survivors from the financial risk of your death. You need sufficient life insurance to ensure that your survivors have enough income to live at the same standard of living that they maintained while you were alive. To determine how much life insurance that you need, you must compute what your survivors' annual income would be without you (current salary, social security benefits, etc.) minus the survivors' estimated living expenses. In addition, you must determine how long they will need this income. This difference is the amount of annual income that your insurance death benefit must provide. Your objective is to purchase sufficient life insurance to meet this financial goal.

- *Disability Insurance*

Disability insurance protects you in the event that you become disabled and cannot work. You pay an annual premium for a disability insurance policy that will pay you a specified sum every month if you become disabled. Most people are much more likely to become disabled than die. However, they do not protect against this risk by purchasing disability insurance. Many financial planners advise people to have approximately 60% of their income covered in the event that they become disabled.

- *Homeowners Insurance*

Homeowners insurance covers the dwelling and the contents of a home. Financial planners typically advise clients to provide coverage for all risks on the dwelling with coverage on specific items in the house. However, the most important thing to know about homeowners insurance is that costs and coverage vary significantly among insurance companies. It is essential that you compare policies among at least three insurers (if not more).

- *Automobile Insurance*

There are five basic coverage areas for most automobile insurance. The first is liability coverage which covers injuries to passengers in your car, other cars, and pedestrians. The second is property damage which covers damage to property caused by the insured car. The third is medical payment coverage which covers medical bills. The fourth is protection from uninsured or under-insured drivers which protects you if you are hit by someone with little or no insurance. The fifth is collision coverage which covers damage to your automobile. Where you live, the condition of your car, the age of the drivers, and the frequency with which you use your car are the key factors in determining your auto insurance coverage needs.

Insurance is an essential component of a financial plan. Early in your career, you may only need health insurance through work and auto insurance for your car. However, if you have a family and buy a house, your insurance strategy will change. Unfortunately, knowing how much insurance to purchase is often confusing. You should do extensive research on the Internet and speak with at least three financial advisors before finalizing an insurance strategy.

3. Create an Investment Strategy

Your investment strategy is the foundation of your financial plan. The right investment strategy can make you very wealthy. The wrong investment strategy can lead to the loss of everything that you own. Your investment strategy should be focused on investing the money that you have over and above what you need to pay your monthly bills (and achieve your liquid savings goals). Investing is very confusing. Many people are turned off by investing because of the large number of complicated investment vehicles available to them. If they are not introduced to investing in the right way, they get frustrated and do not invest their money appropriately.

For many people, the most effective way to begin to understand investing is to learn about mutual funds. Investing in mutual funds is one of the best ways to achieve your financial goals. Unfortunately, most students know very little about mutual funds. A mutual fund is an investment vehicle that uses shareholder's money to purchase a packaged group of investments that achieve a stated investment objective. Most mutual funds invest in stocks and/or bonds. Stocks represent shares of ownership in a company and are the most common investment vehicle traded on securities markets. Companies issue stocks when they are attempting to raise capital (money to invest in their business). Bonds are the lending investments most frequently traded on securities markets. When bonds are issued, they contain a specified maturity date and interest rate. The value of a bond fluctuates based on prevailing interest rates. Their value usually does not fluctuate as much as stocks, so they are typically safer investments. Each share of a mutual fund is priced, based on the value of the stocks and bonds in the mutual fund's portfolio.

Mutual funds are managed by an investment manager who buys and sells stocks and bonds to get the best rate of interest and share price increase for mutual fund shareholders. Mutual funds combine the purchased investments into one portfolio. Investors can buy shares of the mutual fund portfolio at the going rate (often as low as $20 per share). This makes the purchase of mutual funds accessible to people who do not have a lot of money to invest.

Mutual funds were introduced in the United States in the early 1920s. However, the Great Depression severely limited investment in mutual funds until the late 1930s. Since then, the growth in mutual funds has been nothing short of phenomenal. Because of the low cost of investing, investments in mutual funds have grown exponentially over the years. There are three major advantages of investing in mutual funds:

    a) **Inexpensive investment diversification.**
    b) **Professional money management.**
    c) **Easy investing of and access to your money.**

Inexpensive Investment Diversification

Mutual funds enable you to invest in numerous securities (stocks) without a lot of money. Mutual funds will usually invest in 50 or more securities to diversify the investment portfolio. The goal of this diversification is to achieve the highest possible return at the lowest possible risk (within

185

the parameters of the fund's investment objective). To own a portion of this diversified portfolio, all you have to do is buy a mutual fund share. To achieve this kind of diversification on your own, you would have to spend tens of thousands of dollars.

Professional Money Management

Every mutual fund is managed by an investment manager focused on making money for shareholders. This money manager typically manages a team of people who conduct research and analysis aimed at achieving the investment goals of the mutual fund. Moreover, money managers have the added benefit of reduced transaction fees (the costs associated with the buying and selling of stocks) because of the size of their trades. The cost of this professional management is minimal because it is shared by thousands of investors.

Easy Investing of and Access to Your Money

Some mutual funds can be opened for as little as $100 a month. This money can be automatically withdrawn from your checking account each month. Few investments allow the same flexibility in contributions. One of the best features of mutual funds is the access that you have to your money. If you sell mutual fund shares, you will typically receive a check within seven days of the transaction. This feature makes conservative mutual funds excellent investment vehicles for most levels of your FPP.

Investing in mutual funds is an excellent way to invest your money to achieve both long- and short-term financial goals. Early in your career, your investment strategy should be based on investing in different types of mutual funds. However, as your net worth grows and you learn more about investing, you will very likely invest in individual stocks and bonds. Your investment strategy should be focused on reaching a financial investment level that will help you reach a specific goal (i.e. purchase a house, achieve certain retirement income, etc.). The type of mutual funds that you choose to invest in depend on your willingness to take investment risks. You should take time to learn about the potential risk of losing money on each investment that you make. To learn more about mutual funds and investments, you should do extensive research on the Internet.

4. Create a Retirement Strategy

If you live long enough, you will want to retire with sufficient money to live a comfortable life. To achieve this goal, you should develop a retirement strategy that ensures that you save enough money to reach your financial retirement goals. The most common retirement planning mistakes are not starting your retirement planning in your 20s and underestimating the amount of money you will need for retirement. If you invested $2,000 at the beginning of each year and received interest compounded at 8% annually, at age 65, you would have: $98,846 if you started at age 45; $244,692 if you started at age 35; and $559,562 if you started at age 25. Clearly, starting early makes a big difference in your retirement account. People often underestimate the amount of money they need for retirement because they forget to think about the impact of inflation (the gradual reduction of the value of your money over time). The value of $1 (assuming an annual inflation rate of 3%) would be approximately 86 cents in five years, 64 cents in 15 years, and 48 cents in 25 years. You must therefore consider the diminishing value of money in your retirement planning.

One excellent retirement strategy is putting as much money as you can into your company's 401K Plan (or similar retirement plans). These retirement planning vehicles are excellent ways to save a lot of money. Some companies will take money (before taxes are taken out) from your paycheck and invest it in a retirement plan. They may also match a percentage of your contributions (in essence giving you free money) if you stay with the company for 5 years or more. You are allowed to transfer these retirement investments to a personal account even if you leave the company. Your retirement strategy should include a plan to have enough income (taking into account the interest that you will earn and the estimated inflation rate) to allow you to retire comfortably without having to work.

5. Create a Speculation Strategy

Your speculation investment strategy should complement your investment and retirement strategies. Once you have developed and fully funded your liquid savings, protection, investment, and retirement strategies, you can begin to invest in speculative (high-risk) investments. These investments (include the commodity markets, precious metals, very low-priced stocks, and other investments with a potential for a high rate of return or loss) are only for people who are willing to take risks. You should only develop a speculation strategy after you have developed a high net worth and understand your tolerance for taking risks.

6. Develop a Personal Financial Planning Pyramid (FPP)

Now that you know each component of the Personal Financial Planning Pyramid (FPP), you should be able to develop your own FPP. Your first step is to write the total amount of your liquid savings in the base of the pyramid. Your second step is to write down each of the insurance products that you have purchased in the second section of the pyramid. Your third step is to write down each of your investments in the third section of the pyramid. Your fourth step is to write down each of your retirement investments in the fourth section of the pyramid. Your final step is to list any speculative investments that you have (if any) on the fifth step of the pyramid.

See the example for Ted Wilson:

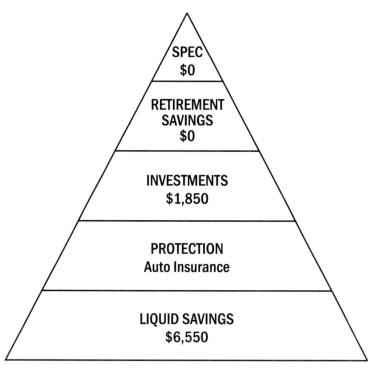

Ted Wilson's Personal
Financial Planning Pyramid June 30, XXXX

As you can see, Ted Wilson has $6,550 in Liquid Savings for bills and emergencies; he has purchased Automobile Insurance; Investments of $1,850; no Retirement Savings; and no money in Speculative investments.

7. *Maintain Excellent Credit*

It is extremely important to maintain an excellent credit record. Credit is primarily determined by the frequency with which you pay your obligations and the amount of total debt that you have. If you focus on paying all your bills on time (or early) and minimizing your debt, you will have excellent credit. One of the keys to maximizing your financial health is having good credit. To purchase a home or other investments, you must have excellent credit. Unfortunately, because many students live beyond their means and abuse their credit cards, their credit is often

189

poor. You should do everything possible to pay your bills on time and maintain excellent credit. In addition, you must review your personal credit report at least once a year to make sure that there are no mistakes on the report.

Credit problems are commonplace to people of all ages. Unfortunately, because credit is so easily accessible, many people spend much more money than they make. Therefore, their personal income statement is negative and they are late paying their bills. The solution to this problem is easy on paper. All you have to do is make sure that you don't spend more than you bring in. However, the purchasing temptations created by effective marketing and easily accessible credit cards make it hard to resist spending beyond your means. The unfortunate reality is that you must be disciplined in your purchases. The only way to address the problem of a negative income statement is to create and follow a monthly budget and pay off your credit cards every month. You must develop the discipline to resist the temptation to spend money on things that you cannot afford. It will be difficult at first. However, once you develop the habit of spending your money responsibly, it will be easy to minimize your debt and maintain excellent credit.

8. Focus on Maximizing Your Net Worth

Your financial plan must be designed to increase your net worth. All too often people are focused on maximizing their salary, not what they are worth. Unfortunately, many people have a negative net worth because they owe more money than they have in assets. They are focused on their income rather than their net worth and don't understand that "it does not matter what you make; all that matters is what you keep." Your income tells very little about your financial success. You can make $1 million a year and still lose money every year because you spend $1.5 million dollars.

You should make financial decisions based on your personal net worth statement because it is the true measure of financial success. In layman's terms, net worth is simply the market value of everything that you own minus all the money that you owe. You must therefore focus on increasing your net worth by increasing your investment savings and minimizing your debts. The earlier that you start to focus on maximizing your net worth, the more likely you will become financially secure at some point in your life.

9. Begin the Process of Tax Planning

The more money you make, the more important tax planning becomes. There are many financial experts who can help you minimize your taxes. However, you do not need to hire them until you earn a very high salary. While you are working on developing a successful career, you should learn as much as you can about federal, state, and local taxes so that you have a basic understanding of tax planning. By conducting a thorough search of the Internet, you will learn a great deal about tax preparation and planning.

10. Develop and Implement Your Financial Plan

Now that you have developed liquid savings, protection, investment, retirement and speculation strategies and defined your financial goals, you are ready to develop your financial plan. Planning for your financial future is a challenging and sometimes confusing task. Your financial plan should be based on 1-year (short-term), 3-year (intermediate-term), and 20-year (long-term) plans for each level of the pyramid. In your 1-year plan, you should estimate what your income and expenses will be in the year. The amount of money that you have available after your expenses are paid (net income) will be used to invest in as many levels of the FPP as possible.

You must have your three to six months of liquid savings and the appropriate insurance before you can invest in the other levels of the pyramid. Consequently, you may not be able to invest in each level of the FPP. However, by beginning your financial plan this way, you will be in a good position to develop solid 3- and 20-year financial plans.

In your 3-year plan, you should develop a plan to invest in every level of the pyramid (except speculation). In your 20-year financial plan, you should develop a strategy to invest in every level of the FPP to achieve a specified net worth goal. Once you have developed these plans, you should implement them by investing the appropriate amount each month necessary to achieve your 1-, 3- and 20-year financial planning goals. This will be a challenge. However, your financial future depends on your ability to achieve these financial planning goals.

Please review the 1-, 3-, and 20-year sample financial planning goals for Ted Wilson as depicted on the Financial Planning Pyramid that follows:

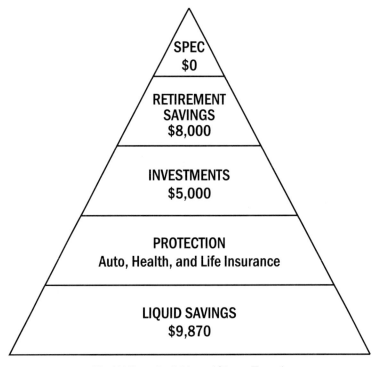

Ted Wilson's 1-Year (Short-Term)
Financial Planning Pyramid Goals

Ted Wilson may have just started a job so his initial focus in his 1-year goal should be on building up his liquid savings, purchasing health and life insurance through work, maximizing his contribution to the company 401K retirement program, and investing money for a house or his education.

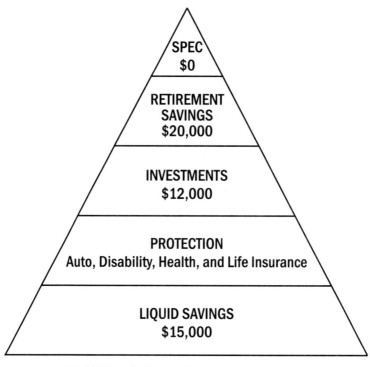

Ted Wilson's 3-Year (Intermediate-Term)
Financial Planning Pyramid Goals

Ted Wilson anticipates working for the same company for the next three years so he knows how much money he will have to invest each month. He therefore invests the same amount every month in the company 401K, several mutual funds, and ensures that his liquid savings account has at least three months' gross income in it. In his financial plan, he will outline how much money he will invest each month into certain investment vehicles to achieve this goal.

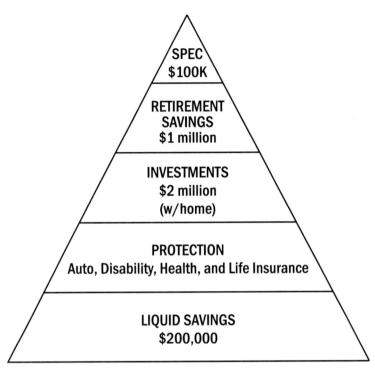

20-Year (Long-Term)
Financial Planning Pyramid Goals

In Ted Wilson's 20-year plan, he can dream a little. He can assume that he has found a successful and financially rewarding career and will consistently invest money every month. He therefore anticipates owning a home, in addition to millions of dollars of investments. In his financial plan, he will list his specific financial goals and outline how much money he will invest each month into certain investment vehicles to achieve these goals. This FPP may seem to be unrealistic. However, if you are focused on careers like entrepreneurship, investment banking, or management consulting, you can easily exceed the numbers listed in this pyramid.

RECOMMENDATION

You are never too young or too poor to develop a financial plan. You may not have much money to invest. However, you can develop financial planning goals and a long-term strategy to achieve these goals. To develop a thorough understanding of your current financial situation, you should develop a budget and determine your net worth as soon as possible. This is the first step in determining your financial health. If you follow the financial planning guidelines in this chapter, you will be well positioned for your financial future. You should complete the FINANCIAL PLANNING PREPARATION QUESTIONNAIRE to assess your readiness to develop a financial plan.

FINANCIAL PLANNING PREPARATION QUESTIONNAIRE

This questionnaire should inspire you to comprehensively prepare for the development of a financial plan. Please answer the following financial planning preparation questions by circling either *Yes* or *No*.

1. Do you understand what financial planning is? **Yes** **No**

2. Have you determined your monthly and annual income? **Yes** **No**

3. Have you determined your monthly and annual expenses? **Yes** **No**

4. Have you reviewed in detail your latest federal and state tax returns? **Yes** **No**

5. Have you listed the value of your assets? **Yes** **No**

6. Have you listed your total liabilities? **Yes** **No**

7. Have you created your personal budget and income statement? **Yes** **No**

8. Have you created a personal net worth statement? **Yes** **No**

9. Have you written down your financial goals? **Yes** **No**

10. Do you understand the Financial Planning Pyramid (FPP)? **Yes** **No**

These questions should force you to reflect on the things that you need to do to prepare for the development of a financial plan. If you answered "Yes" to each of these questions, then you should be ready to develop a financial plan. However, if you answered "No" to one or more of these questions, you should make a special effort to do the financial planning preparation that you are not doing. You should continue to work on these things until you can accurately answer "Yes" to every question. Once you have done this, you are ready to complete the FINANCIAL PLANNING CHECKLIST below.

FINANCIAL PLANNING CHECKLIST

The list below contains each of the things that you should do to complete a comprehensive financial plan. Please check each of the items that you have completed below:

1. _____ I have completed my liquid savings strategy.

2. _____ I have completed my insurance strategy.

3. _____ I have completed my investment strategy.

4. _____ I have completed my retirement strategy.

5. _____ I have completed my speculation strategy.

6. _____ I have developed my personal Financial Planning Pyramid.

7. _____ I am maintaining excellent credit.

8. _____ I am attempting to maximize my net worth.

9. _____ I have begun the process of tax planning.

10. _____ I have developed and implemented my financial plan.

By completing each of the ten things on this checklist, you have completed the process of developing a financial plan. If there are items on this list that you are not able to check off because you have not done them, you should do them as soon as possible. You will significantly enhance your chances of financial success if you do each of the things on the FINANCIAL PLANNING CHECKLIST.

CHAPTER 17

What Is Investing and Why Is It Important?

Ten Rules of Investing

One of the most important components of your financial plan is your investment strategy. A well thought-out long-term investment strategy can help you save enough money to buy a house or retire comfortably. A comprehensive short-term investment plan can help you pay for college, buy a car to get to work, or meet some other important need that can further your career. No matter what your financial needs are, you should follow the Ten Rules of Investing:

1. Start early.
2. Learn how to read investment information.
3. Know how much to invest.
4. Understand compound interest.
5. Know the Rule of 72.
6. Explore your investment options.
7. Maximize the use of company retirement plans.
8. Take advantage of dollar-cost averaging.
9. Develop an investment plan.
10. Implement an investment plan.

1. Start Early

You should begin to develop and implement your investment plan as early in your life as possible. The earlier that you start to develop the habit of saving, the more likely you will be to achieve your financial goals. For example, if you are able to save $300 a month at age 25 and you get a 9% after-tax return on your money, you will have approximately $336,337 at age 50. However, if you save $300 a month at age 40 and you get a 9% after-tax return, you will have approximately $58,054 at age 50. By waiting 15 years, you will lose $278,283 in potential investments. You should therefore start saving your money today.

2. Learn How To Read Investment Information

Make every effort to learn how to read the financial section of the largest newspaper in your area. Look at the section of the paper that lists each of the companies on the New York Stock Exchange (NYSE). Find the names of companies that you know and write down their stock symbol, their current stock price, their 52-week high and low (if it is listed), and the one-day increase or decrease. You should also look at the listing of different mutual funds. Write down the different prices of the funds and their change from the previous day. You should pick some stocks and mutual funds and track their prices for a month to get a feel for the fluctuation of investments. Also, read relevant articles on the markets and investing in general. The more you read the financial section of newspapers, the more comfortable you will become investing your money.

3. Know How Much To Invest

It is surprisingly easy to become addicted to investing. Once you invest some money and you start to see it grow, you can catch an "investing bug" where you put more money than you can afford into investments. This can be dangerous because you may dip into your liquid savings and not have enough cash available to pay for emergencies. For example, stocks can be great investments. However, they are not considered liquid because you risk losing significant amounts of money if you are forced to sell stocks before you want to (to meet emergency needs). You should therefore only invest money in individual stocks after you have satisfied the financial requirements of your liquid savings, protection, investment, and retirement financial plans. The amount of money that you invest is simply that amount required to meet the goals of your 1-year financial plan.

4. Understand Compound Interest

One of the main reasons to start investing early is because of the incredible benefits of compound interest. If someone offered you the following choice: work for 35 days at a salary of $100,000 per day or work for 1 cent the first day and double the payment each subsequent day (i.e. 2 cents the second day, 4 cents the third day, etc.), which scenario would you choose? Most people would choose to work for 35 days at a salary of $100,000 per day. Unfortunately, most people don't understand the power of compounding. By working for 35 days at a salary of $100,000, you would receive $3,500,000. However, because of compounding, the second choice would bring you more than $339,000,000, making you $335,500,000 richer than those people who do not understand the power of compounding. Likewise, compound interest increases exponentially so your return on an investment accelerates rapidly. By investing a regular amount every month as early in your life as possible, you will be able to significantly increase your net worth over time because of the power of compound interest.

5. Know the Rule of 72

What if you don't have a calculator and someone asks you the following question: "I have $10,000 to invest. How long will it take my money to double at a 12% interest rate?" Most people would say: "I have no idea!" Most good financial planners would simply refer to the Rule of 72 and say, "Approximately six years."

The Rule of 72 basically tells you that if you divide the interest rate that you anticipate receiving on an investment by 72, you will get the approximate number of years that it will take for that investment to double. For example, if you have a certain amount of money to invest and you anticipate that you can get a 10% interest rate, then your money will double in 7.2 years.

Why is the Rule of 72 important? It is an excellent way to quickly determine what you need to invest to achieve your financial goals. Imagine that you want to buy a house in six years. You estimate that you will need $40,000 for the down payment on the house. However, you only have $20,000 saved for the house. Now that you know the Rule of 72, you recognize that you will have to find an investment that will provide a 12% annual interest rate to double your money in six years.

---

6. Explore Your Investment Options

The great variety of investments available to you can make investing very confusing. You should therefore begin investing in mutual funds until you feel comfortable with other investment vehicles. Mutual funds continue to be the most popular investment used to achieve personal financial planning goals. There are many different types of mutual funds. However, in general terms, there are the following three major types:

- a) **Money market mutual funds**
- b) **Bond funds**
- c) **Stock funds**

Money Market Mutual Funds

Money market mutual funds are the only type of mutual fund in which the share price is locked at $1 per share and does not vary. Owners of money market mutual funds receive dividend payments. These funds are attractive because the dividend payment is typically higher than the interest you would receive in a bank savings account. In addition, money market mutual funds usually provide shareholders with check writing privileges (although checks usually have to be $250 or more). Money market mutual funds are usually not insured. However, they invest large sums of money in Treasury Securities and other government debt; 60- to 90-day commercial paper (short-term debt issued by major corporations); and large certificates of deposit (CDs).

Bond Funds

Like money market mutual funds, bond funds are considered one of the safest types of mutual funds. Bond funds invest in bonds issued by corporations and governments. Bond mutual funds contain a diversified portfolio of many bonds, thereby minimizing the risk to shareholders. Each bond has a specified interest rate and maturity date. Typically, fund managers will hold a wide variety of bonds with many different interest rates and maturity dates to increase the investment return while minimizing the investment risk.

The three types of bond funds are "Short-term," "Intermediate Term," and "Long-term." Short-term bond fund managers purchase bonds that are maturing in the next few years. Intermediate-term bond fund managers purchase bonds that mature in seven to ten years. Long-term bond fund managers purchase bonds that mature in fifteen or more years. The bond funds purchasing longer-term bonds will typically fluctuate more in price and have a higher rate of return.

The rate of return of bond funds also depends on the credit rating of the bonds. The lower the credit rating, the greater the risk of default and the higher the interest rate. Some funds invest in only AAA- and AA-rated bonds. Other funds invest in BB- or lower-rated bonds. All bond funds are not the same. Make sure that you understand what bonds are in a mutual fund portfolio before you invest in bond funds.

Stock Funds

Stocks represent a share of ownership in a corporation. Stock funds invest mostly in the stocks of publicly traded companies. Stock funds are the most popular of all mutual funds because they have outpaced inflation by 10% to 20% (some funds have done even better) over the last 20 years. Money market mutual funds and bond funds are much safer investments; however, they have outpaced inflation by only 3% to 5% in the same time period. Stock fund managers purchase a portfolio of stocks that they believe will help them achieve their investment goals while minimizing their investment risk.

Stock funds make money through dividends, capital gains distributions, and appreciation. Some of the stocks within a mutual fund portfolio pay dividends which are passed on to the mutual fund shareholder. The profit received from selling a stock at a higher price than the purchased price is called "capital gains." These capital gains (or capital losses) are shared by the mutual fund shareholders. The mutual fund purchase price per share fluctuates on a daily basis.

Investing in stock funds has proven to be one of the best ways to achieve your financial goals. However, each stock mutual fund has a specific investment objective. Before investing, it is important that you understand the different investment objectives of stock mutual funds. The major stock mutual fund objectives and the generally used fund objective codes (listed in parenthesis) include the following:

- **Balanced (BL):** Invests in conservative stocks and bonds.
- **Capital Appreciation (CA):** Focused on achieving rapid capital growth by frequently buying and selling stocks.
- **Emerging Markets (EM):** Contains stocks of emerging companies.
- **Equity Income (EI):** Invests in stocks with the highest dividend income.
- **Global (GL):** Contains international and United States-based stocks.
- **Gold (AU):** Usually invests in gold mines, bullion, and coins.
- **Growth (GR):** Contains stocks that can potentially yield above-average revenue and earnings growth.
- **Growth & Income (GI):** Contains stocks that will achieve higher than average price and dividend income growth.
- **International (IL):** Invests only in international stocks.
- **Mid-Cap (MC):** Invests in stocks of middle-sized companies.
- **Small Cap (SC):** Contains stocks of smaller companies.

This is by no means a complete list of fund types. However, in this list, the Balanced and Equity Income mutual funds are typically the least risky funds. The Emerging Markets, Global, Gold, International, Sector and Small Cap mutual funds tend to be the most risky funds.

The best way to begin developing an investment portfolio is to review the mutual fund listings of a major newspaper and track mutual funds with different investment objectives. This approach helps you learn how to read mutual fund quotations and become comfortable with mutual fund investing. Moreover, you will better understand the risks associated with certain types of mutual funds without investing any money. At first, mutual fund investing may sound complicated. However, after reading the mutual fund listings for a few weeks, it will become second nature. Start looking at the paper today. The sooner you start reviewing mutual fund listings, the sooner you will become comfortable investing in mutual funds.

7. Maximize the Use of Company Investment Plans

You should take full advantage of your 401K or the other retirement savings accounts available to you at work. Ideally, you should save at least 10%-15% of your income each year for retirement. (Don't rely on Social Security as your sole means of retirement income.) 401K plans make saving for retirement very easy. Most companies have a 401K plan that enables you to have up to 15% of your pre-tax income (within federal maximums) taken out of your paycheck. In addition, many companies will contribute 25 cents for every dollar that you contribute up to 6% of your salary. This free money is yours if you stay with the company for a specified period of time (frequently five years). If you leave within five years, only the money you contributed and the interest on this money are yours.

The money taken out of your paycheck is often less than the amount that you are contributing because this amount may reduce your tax bracket and thereby reduce tax deductions from your paycheck. For example, if you contribute $10,000 a year to your 401K plan, your net paycheck may be reduced by only $9,000. Best of all, this money can be used before you retire. You can borrow 50% of the money saved in your 401K to purchase a house or pay emergency bills. However, there are financial penalties if you do not pay this money back. Maximizing your retirement savings at work is one of the easiest and most profitable ways to save money.

8. Take Advantage of Dollar-Cost Averaging

Dollar-cost averaging is one of the best benefits of investing in mutual funds because it is simple and usually effective. All you have to do is invest the same dollar amount in the same mutual fund every month. The benefit of doing this is that you are guaranteed to buy more shares when a mutual fund price is lower and fewer shares when the mutual fund price is higher. Historically, dollar-cost averaging has enabled many mutual fund investors to benefit because of the fluctuation of the price of mutual funds.

For example, if you invest $100 in a month and the price of the mutual fund is $10 per share, then you buy 10 shares the first month. If the price of the mutual fund drops to $5 a share in the second month, then you buy 20 mutual fund shares. Finally, if the price of the mutual fund goes back to $10 per share, you buy another 10 mutual fund shares. You now have a total of 40 mutual fund shares (10 plus 20 plus 10) worth $400 (40 times $10). However, you only invested $300. Because of dollar-cost averaging, you were able to increase the value of your mutual fund portfolio, even though the price of your mutual fund never went above your purchase price. Dollar-cost averaging does not guarantee that you make money. However, over time, it has proven to be a good way to invest your money in mutual funds.

9. Develop an Investment Plan

In your financial plan, you developed a general investment strategy. However, before you can begin to make investments, you should develop a detailed investment plan. In this plan, you will specify exactly where you will invest your money (after you have made the necessary liquid savings and protection investments). You may want 25% of your money invested in safe stock or bond mutual funds; you may want 30% of your money invested in international mutual funds; 35% of your money in growth mutual funds; and 10% of your money invested in small cap mutual funds. Your investment plan can be any combination of investments that you think will meet your personal objectives. Your investment plan will tell you how you should diversify your investments to maximize your return and minimize your risk.

10. Implement an Investment Plan

Once your investment plan has been completed, you should begin to invest your money. Ideally, you will invest the same amount of money every month as early in your career as possible. The regular investments will enable you to take advantage of dollar-cost averaging. Early investing will enable you to take advantage of compound interest. You will find that over time the value of your investments will fluctuate. However, it usually makes sense to "stay the course" if you are investing for the long-term.

RECOMMENDATION

You should learn as much as you can about investing as early in your life as possible. Do not wait until you have money to invest to start researching investments. If you take the time to read the financial section of a major paper and search the Internet for information, you will learn more than enough to make informed investments. However, it will take time to become a savvy investor. Investing can be a lot of fun. Typically, the sooner you start investing, the more successful you will be at managing your money. You may even enjoy investing so much that you will want to pursue a career as a financial planner or investment banker. You should complete the following INVESTING QUESTIONNAIRE to determine how prepared you are to start investing.

INVESTING QUESTIONNAIRE

This questionnaire should inspire you to do the preparation necessary to invest. Please answer the investing questions below by circling either *Yes* or *No*.

1. Do you understand why it is important to start investing early? **Yes No**

2. Do you know how to read investment information? **Yes No**

3. Do you know how much you should invest? **Yes No**

4. Do you understand compound interest? **Yes No**

5. Do you understand the Rule of 72? **Yes No**

6. Have you explored all of your investment options? **Yes No**

7. Have you maximized the use of your company's retirement programs? **Yes No**

8. Do you understand Dollar Cost Averaging? **Yes No**

9. Have you developed an investment plan? **Yes No**

10. Have you implemented an investment plan? **Yes No**

These questions should motivate you to learn as much as you can about investing. If you answered "Yes" to each of these questions, then you are ready to begin investing. However, if you answered "No" to one or more of these questions, you should make a special effort to do further research on investing. You should continue to work on these things until you can accurately answer "Yes" to every question.

CHAPTER 18

Now That I Am Working, How Do I Manage My Life?

Managing Your Life

The wonderful thing about succeeding in a career is that you enjoy going to work every day. In addition, you have the benefit of having enough money to pay your bills and invest. The challenge about succeeding in a career is that you may have trouble managing your life because you will be spending so much time at work. You will likely not be able to interact with friends or participate in leisure activities as often as you would like. You may also find it challenging to develop romantic relationships or visit your family. However, there are ten rules of life management that can help you effectively address these challenges:

1. Set your personal goals.
2. Take time for yourself.
3. Develop an errand plan.
4. Keep in touch.
5. Make your social life a priority.
6. Value family relationships.
7. Have a fun budget.
8. Develop a vacation plan.
9. Maintain your mental and physical health.
10. Schedule your week.

1. Set Your Personal Goals

In order to accomplish anything significant, you must set goals. It is important to set career goals. However, it is also extremely important to set personal goals. A personal goal is an objective that you would like to accomplish that is unrelated to work. Now that you are working, you have limited free time. You must therefore prioritize your time in a way that will enable you to achieve your personal goals. If you enjoy exercising, travel, or various forms of entertainment, you should set personal goals that will enable you to spend as much time as possible doing what you enjoy. Ideally, you should list your five most important personal goals. For example, if spending time with friends and family, playing tennis, going to concerts, and travel are most important to you, then your list would be as follows:

a) **Spending time with friends**
b) **Visiting with family**
c) **Playing tennis**
d) **Going to concerts**
e) **Travel**

Once you have set your personal goals, you should develop weekly, monthly, and yearly plans that will enable you to achieve your goals.

2. Take Time for Yourself

The demands of work and life can be overwhelming. It is therefore important to take time to relax and stimulate your sense of self. You should schedule time to regularly sit in silence, meditate, or read to connect with yourself. If you do not schedule time for yourself, you will probably feel a sense of dissatisfaction with your life. You may feel tired, depressed, angry, frustrated, and unproductive largely because you are consumed by the responsibilities of work and life. The stress of work, combined with the pressures of social activities, can be overwhelming. To deal with this stress, you should focus on relaxing and reflecting. Some people find that taking a long shower, reading a book, or meditating regularly provide the relaxation that they need to rejuvenate themselves. You should schedule time daily or weekly to spend time with yourself in an enjoyable way.

3. Develop an Errand Plan

If you are like most people, you have many weekly errands to do. You may need to clean your home, buy groceries, do laundry, deposit money in the bank, and accomplish many other personal chores every week. These chores can consume your entire free time if you do not schedule them. Completing errands is typically not a lot of fun. You should therefore develop an errand plan to schedule each of your chores in a way that maximizes your free time. It is important to schedule these errands by the minute to ensure that you are able to complete as many errands as possible in the minimum amount of time. For example, your errand plan may require that you do your laundry at 8 a.m., go to the bank at 8:45 a.m., and clean your apartment at 9:40 a.m. If you can accomplish these errands on schedule, you will have more time to do what you enjoy. It is much easier to develop an errand plan than to follow one. To ensure that you complete all your necessary errands, you should do everything you can to complete your errands on time.

4. Keep in Touch

When you have a demanding job, it is very easy to lose touch with your friends and family. You may forget to call or email them because you are consumed with the demands of work. Your friends and family obviously can help you have fun and provide needed stress relief. However, they also represent an important support network and advisory group that can provide critical career and life advice. The pressures of work can be overwhelming. It is important that you speak with people regularly who have your best interest in mind when offering advice. Your friends and family can help you make important career and life decisions because they sometimes know you better than you know yourself. You should therefore make every effort to speak with your close friends and family members at least once a week. If you do not have time to get together with them or call them, you should send them an email. People understand that, when you have a demanding job, you may have less time to get together. However, there is no excuse for not keeping in touch by phone or email. In addition, at a minimum, you should get together with close friends and family members at least once a month.

5. Make Your Social Life a Priority

It is great to keep in touch with your friends. However, it is even more important to get together with them to socialize. You will be more successful in your career if you are able to interact regularly with your close friends. This interaction will help to rejuvenate you when you are facing the inevitable challenges of work. For most people, it is also important to have a girlfriend, boyfriend, (wife or husband) in their lives. This intimate personal relationship provides the most valuable support and advice network possible. The best way to meet a potential girlfriend or boyfriend is to have a vibrant social life. You should therefore make your social life a priority in spite of the demands of work.

6. Value Family Relationships

Typically, your most reliable support network is your family. Your friends often come in and out of your life. However, your family members will always be related to you and, in most cases, have an interest in your well-being. In addition, family members usually feel more comfortable telling you the truth (even if it hurts your feelings). Sometimes their brutal honesty is exactly what you need to make important business and life decisions. You should therefore attempt to spend time with close family members as often as you possibly can.

7. Have a Fun Budget

Having fun is a very important aspect of life. Unfortunately, having fun usually costs money. You may want to treat your family to dinner, go to a concert with friends, or visit an exotic travel destination. However, you cannot do these things without setting aside money to pay for these fun activities. The best way to do this is to create a fun budget. In this budget, you should list all the fun things that you want to do and assign a cost to each of them. The total cost is your dream fun budget. You will probably not be able to afford to do everything in this budget. You should therefore pick as many fun activities as possible that fit within your total personal budget. Including fun activities in your personal budget will enable you to maximize the number of enjoyable things that you can do each week.

8. Develop a Vacation Plan

Everybody needs to take vacation. They need to get away from work to spend time with their family and friends without the pressures of work. You should therefore always take every vacation day available to you. Most organizations understand that their employees need vacation to maximize their productivity at work. Unfortunately, many people wait until the last minute to plan their vacation. They therefore have few vacation options because of high costs and limited availability. You should carefully plan your vacation each year to maximize the enjoyment that you get from your time away from work. Take the time to research every potential vacation option that appeals to you. You should pick the vacation destinations that will provide the most enjoyment at a price that fits within your personal budget. A carefully planned vacation will significantly enhance your enjoyment of life and performance at work.

9. Maintain Your Mental and Physical Health

You will only be happy if you are mentally and physically healthy. Your emotional, rational, and physical well-being is the key to your enjoyment of life and success at work. You should enhance your emotional health by improving your personal emotional awareness, emotional self-control, emotional sensitivity, and emotional leadership. In addition, you should set emotional health goals. You should improve your rational health by maximizing your knowledge, enhancing your analytical skills, refining your communication skills, using your intelligence, and setting rational health goals. You should enhance your physical health goals by eating properly, exercising regularly, maximizing your blood health, and setting physical health goals.

10. Schedule Your Week

The only way to effectively manage your life is to schedule all your major weekly activities. In addition to your work schedule, you should schedule time for yourself, social activities, family visits, recreation, and other activities that will enhance your mental and physical health. This planning will enable you to manage both your time and your life effectively. You will find that a schedule will prevent you from wasting time on unproductive activities. The schedule will also allow you to have control over your life. Initially, you may find it difficult to schedule your week. However, after developing four to five weekly schedules, you will probably develop the ability to effectively schedule your week and begin the process of successfully managing your life.

RECOMMENDATION

Excelling in work and life is not easy. The demands of a job can prevent you from effectively managing your life. The challenges caused by problems with family and/or friends can negatively impact the quality of your work. To succeed in work and life, you must set personal goals that allow you to have time for yourself; connect with friends and family; complete personal errands; and, enhance your mental and physical health. To assess how well you are managing your life, you should complete the following LIFE MANAGEMENT QUESTIONNAIRE.

LIFE MANAGEMENT QUESTIONNAIRE

This questionnaire should inspire you to do the things necessary to effectively manage your life. Please answer the life management questions below by circling either *Yes* or *No*.

1. Are you setting realistic personal goals? **Yes   No**

2. Are you taking time for yourself? **Yes   No**

3. Have you developed an errand plan? **Yes   No**

4. Are you keeping in touch with family and friends? **Yes   No**

5. Are you making your social life a priority? **Yes   No**

6. Are you spending enough time with your family? **Yes   No**

7. Do you have a fun budget? **Yes   No**

8. Have you developed a vacation plan? **Yes   No**

9. Are you enhancing your mental and physical health on a weekly basis? **Yes   No**

10. Are you developing a written schedule every week? **Yes   No**

These questions should motivate you to think about managing your life. If you answered "Yes" to each of these questions, then you are well on your way to effective life management. However, if you answered "No" to one or more of these questions, you should make a special effort to work on these things until you can accurately answer "Yes" to every question.

CHAPTER 19

Why Should I Vote?

Why Students Don't Vote

Once you reach the legal voting age, you should make a special effort to vote in every election that you can. Your vote really does matter. Unfortunately, many students take their citizenship for granted. They are unaware of the blood, sweat, and tears that have been shed to create their country and give them the right to vote. These students do not know that citizens in many countries around the world are denied the privilege of voting. They don't understand that elected leaders at the local, state, and federal level play an important role in determining the quality of their life. Consequently, they do not take the time to learn about the key issues facing their country and community and do not vote. There are five main reasons that students don't vote. These are:

a) They don't think that their vote matters.
b) They don't understand the process.
c) They don't understand the different levels of government.
d) They know very little about the candidates.
e) They don't want to take time to vote.

They Don't Think That Their Vote Matters

Many students think that their vote is only important if it breaks an election tie. Since most elections are not close, they think that their vote is usually irrelevant. Incredibly, elections are decided by one vote more often than most people think. There are many election horror stories where a candidate loses an election by one vote because a friend or family member did not think that their vote mattered. Even if an election is not close, your vote matters because the volume of a candidate's victory is important. If the candidate that you vote for wins by a large margin, they will have more of a mandate to make the changes that you want them to make.

They Don't Understand the Process

The election process is very confusing to first-time participants. Many students do not know anything about different political parties, registering to vote, or political issues. They therefore don't vote because they are confused by the different aspects of the political process. However, if you take the time to learn about voting, you will discover that it is easy to understand how elections work. Once you understand the process, you will discover that actively participating in the elections process can be a lot of fun.

They Don't Understand the Different Levels of Government

Unfortunately, most people are not familiar with the multiple levels of government. They often do not know the difference between a member of their local city council or a member of the state legislature. Most students do not know the name of their mayor, congressperson, or Vice-President of the United States. The multiple levels of government are very confusing at first. However, if you take the time to visit the websites of the local, county, state, and federal governments, you will learn about these very different forms of government. This research should make you a lot more comfortable with the concept of voting for candidates running for positions in the different levels of government.

They Know Very Little About the Candidates

It is often difficult to understand what each candidate for office really believes. However, once you learn about the different levels of government, you are ready to research each of the candidates running for office. Usually there is very little information about potential candidates for office until an election is just a few months away. However, when an election is near, you will be bombarded with campaign information. At a minimum, you should visit each candidate's website to learn about their background and the issues they are supporting.

They Don't Want To Take Time To Vote

Unfortunately, because many students are confused about the process and don't understand the importance of voting, they do not think that taking time to vote is worthwhile. They would rather be studying, spending time with friends, or relaxing than going to vote. Many students therefore refuse to register to vote and do not take the time to vote. They miss the chance to impact their communities and support or change certain policies. These students don't realize that it does not take much time to vote. All you have to do is register to vote well before an election and go to your local polling place to cast a vote for your favorite candidates. If you do not vote, you should not complain about elected politicians or the programs and policies they are pursuing. For example, suppose you are concerned about the cost of tuition at a taxpayer-funded university and one candidate supports reducing the cost of college tuition. If you did not take the time to vote for the candidate who supports a reduction in tuition and he or she loses, you should not be surprised when tuition rises. In essence, when you do not vote, you give up the most fundamental right of citizenship. Voting is easier than ever before. Even if you are out of town when voting takes place, you can vote at your convenience though an absentee ballot. There really is no excuse for someone of voting age not to vote.

Why Students SHOULD Vote

Voting provides students with an incredible opportunity to learn about important issues and to influence how government is run. Once you reach

217

voting age, you should take voting as seriously as you would completing a paper for school. You should do extensive research on the key issues and candidates in the election. You should take time to understand the voting process. Most importantly, you should take the time to go to the polls and vote. There are ten main reasons why you should participate in the political process and vote. These are:

1. You can influence other students.
2. The election results will impact your life.
3. Your demographic group will get attention.
4. Registering to vote sends a message.
5. Voting motivates you to learn about the candidates.
6. Voting inspires you to understand key issues.
7. You will help yourself and others.
8. Voting is the benefit of citizenship.
9. You will pay tribute to those who died for the right to vote.
10. You may find a career focus.

1. You Can Influence Other Students

Most students of voting age do not know how much power the right to vote gives them. They focus on the ability of their single vote to make a difference. However, they ignore the influence that they have on others. If you are a student of voting age, you should take advantage of your potential influence. Chances are that many other students feel the way you do about political issues that affect them. However, they are probably apathetic about voting. By telling them who you are voting for and why, you can influence hundreds of people to vote. For example, many students in college would like to be able to get larger government-subsidized student loans at lower interest rates. They therefore would vote for the candidate that supports an increase in this type of financial aid for students. If you tell them you are voting for a candidate for this reason, you can possibly convince them to take the time to vote. Your one vote can potentially become hundreds of votes.

2. The Election Results Will Impact Your Life

People underestimate the impact that election results will have on their life. They assume that their vote does not matter. However, the politicians who are elected can have an incredibly positive or negative effect on everyone's life. Politicians decide how much you will pay in taxes, whether you will go to war, how much is invested in public education, the strength of the economy, and how much your health care costs among other things. They will promote policies that can increase or decrease your tuition or your chances of getting a job. The influence that politicians have on your life is incredible. You should therefore have a strong interest in voting to ensure that the politicians who are elected will make your life easier, not harder.

3. Your Demographic Group Will Get Attention

The government does not track who you are voting for. However, they do know how many people in your demographic group voted. For example, they can track how many people under 21 years of age voted, how many people in your college town voted, etc. By voting and getting your classmates to vote, you will increase the number of students voting for a particular candidate. Groups that have a large number of votes will get strong support from the politicians they elect. Senior citizens (people over 65) vote in a very high percentage. The politicians that they help to elect make it a priority to support the issues that senior citizens care about. Issues like government-supported retirement income, prescription drug costs, and reducing crime are major national issues largely because senior citizens have supported candidates that care about these issues. Likewise, if young people voted in similar numbers, issues like low cost college education and affordable student loans would be major national issues. They currently are not major issues largely because students do not vote in large numbers.

4. Registering To Vote Sends a Message

By registering to vote in large numbers, students will get the attention of major candidates. Early in an election, political candidates review the voter registration rolls to determine who is eligible to vote. If large numbers of students are registered to vote, candidates will develop policy positions that are of interest to students. They will spend time meeting with students and pay more attention to the issues that are of concern to people in high school and college. It is therefore very important that students in your school register to vote in large numbers to attract the interest of political candidates.

5. Voting Motivates You To Learn About the Candidates

If you decide to vote, you should be motivated to do research on each of the candidates in the election. You should review the campaign literature that they distribute, review each candidate's website, and, if possible, speak with each candidate to find out more about what they want to do in office. You will probably enjoy this candidate research process and learn a great deal about government.

6. Voting Inspires You To Understand Key Issues

The purpose of the election process is to identify candidates who will advance the issues that improve the quality of life for residents. There are multiple candidates for every office because people disagree on the issues that will improve resident's quality of life. Some candidates believe that to increase the quality of life for residents, there must be more government influence; others believe in supporting corporations to accomplish this goal while others believe that nonprofits are the key to quality-of-life issues. By choosing to vote, you will be inspired to study each of the major election issues and identify those issues that are most important to you. Ideally, you will vote for the candidate that is most supportive of the issues that are important to you.

7. You Will Help Yourself and Others

By voting, you are expressing your belief that the candidate that you are voting for has the passion and ability to do what you think should be done to help you and other people. If you vote for a candidate that turns out to be very effective, then you will have played an important role in helping yourself and others. If you really believe in this candidate's ability to make positive change, then you may want to volunteer in his or her office. You may even want to apply for a job in the office. Voting is just the first step in helping others. The more you do to help elected officials accomplish their objectives, the more successful you will be in helping yourself and others.

8. Voting Is the Benefit of Citizenship

In countries that have fair and open election processes, it is very easy to complain about the elected officials in the country. Every day there is someone somewhere complaining about the government. However, these people often do not understand that they have the right to complain because of the democratic election process. In many countries around the world where there is no fair and open election process, people are arrested if they are heard complaining about the government. They are often thrown in jail for years simply because they did not blindly praise their political leaders. Unfortunately, in the United States and other countries where people have the right to vote in fair elections, citizenship is frequently not valued. People take for granted their right to vote. You should show that you value your rights as a citizen by voting for the candidate of your choice and becoming active in the political process.

9. You Will Pay Tribute to Those Who Died for the Right to Vote

Most students should know that the 13th, 14th, and 15th Amendments to the U.S. Constitution, which outlawed slavery and extended civil and voting rights to former slaves, were passed in the 1860s. Students should also know that women were not given the right to vote in America until the 19th Amendment to the Constitution was passed in 1920. However, many students do not know that there were many restrictions that prevented African-Americans from voting until the passage of the Voting Rights Act in the 1960s. They may not know that the 26th Amendment to the Constitution lowered the voting age from 21 to 18 in the 1970s because, at the time, 18-year-olds could go to war but could not vote. Unfortunately, many men and women of all races gave their lives in the fight to allow African-Americans and women to vote. In addition, even today, there are people in many countries fighting for the right to vote. By voting, students pay tribute to the many people around the world who died in the fight for voting rights.

10. You May Find a Career Focus

Many people have found great success in careers in government and politics. They have focused their working lives on excelling in jobs in local, county, state, or federal government. Others have done extremely well as politicians, political staff, or as campaign managers. These positions are not for everyone. They require some very unique skills and interests. However, if you thoroughly research government and politics, you may find that you have a passion for pursuing one or more of these careers.

RECOMMENDATION

To fully exercise your right of citizenship, you should take time to register to vote, study the major issues, learn about the political process, find out as much as you can about the candidates for office, and vote. Voting is easy. However, this research may take some time. It will be extremely worthwhile because it will increase your interest in current events, teach you how politics and government work, and enable you to learn how to impact public policy.

As you learn more about the political process, you may find it difficult to determine which candidate to support. Unfortunately, many people vote for the candidate they like based on personality, not on the issues that the candidate is supporting. The ISSUE PREFERENCE RANKING© (IPR) will help you decide which issues are most important to you. Ideally, you should support the candidate whose political priorities are most like your own.

ISSUE PREFERENCE RANKING

The following political issues are listed in random order. Read through each of these issues and rank, in order of importance (1-20), the political issues that are important to you.

A. ____Reducing Taxes

B. ____Ending Poverty

C. ____Funding College Education

D. ____Increasing Government-Funded Retirement Income

E. ____Protecting Civil Rights

F. ____Improving Public School Education

G. ____Reducing Crime

H. ____Strengthening the Military

I. ____Improving Health Care

J. ____ Maintaining a Strong Economy

K. ____ Domestic Security

L. ____Quality Housing for Everyone

M. ____Increasing Employment Opportunities

N. ____Reducing the Size of Government

O. ____Protecting the Environment

P. ____Spreading Global Democracy

Q. ____Immigration

R. ____Empowering Nonprofits

S. ____Ensuring the Separation between Government and Religion

T. ____World Peace

You will probably find that ranking these issues is extremely difficult. It is hard to prioritize so many important issues. Unfortunately, many of these issues compete against each other so it is impossible to accomplish every one of them at the same time. Politicians have the extremely difficult task of deciding what issues to support.

By completing this ranking, you will have a better idea of your personal political preferences. If you don't understand some of these issues, you should discuss them with friends and family, research them in the school library, and do an Internet information search. Once you have ranked these issues, you should study the positions of candidates running for local, county, state, and national office and vote for those candidates who have similar political priorities. Approaching the voting process in this way will help you take full advantage of the incredible power of voting.

CHAPTER 20

Why Should I Help Others?

The Ten Rules of Helping Others

Throughout your career, you should do everything you can to help others. Many people are singularly focused on improving the quality of their life with little concern for others. They develop a laser focus on satisfying their goals and objectives, and ignore the needs of the less fortunate. Unfortunately, the world is filled with people who are suffering. Millions of people are homeless, hungry, illiterate, lonely, and mentally or physically ill. They are in need of financial and human support. They often never get a chance to interact with people like you who are working hard to succeed at work and life. You should therefore do all that you can to take time out of your busy schedule to help people who are suffering. You will get more out of this help than the individuals you are helping. Many people believe that their life only takes on meaning when they help someone who is suffering. You should strive to live a meaningful life by helping others.

You should also go out of your way to give advice to people who experience work challenges that are similar to challenges that you have faced. The only way that you will be successful in your career is if someone helps you. You should therefore "Pay This Help Forward" by helping others succeed. The Ten Rules of Helping Others are these:

1. Pay attention to your work environment.
2. Help co-workers.
3. Understand the problems in your community.
4. Give back to your community.
5. Pay attention to world problems.
6. Develop an interest in the civic sector.
7. Identify specific nonprofits to support.
8. Volunteer your time regularly.
9. Give money.
10. Encourage other people to give back.

---

1. Pay Attention to Your Work Environment

You should develop a sensitivity to the dynamics of your work place. Some of your co-workers may have difficulty completing their assignments on time. Other workers may have abusive bosses, health issues, or transportation issues. Someone in your work place may have recently lost someone close to them. Amazingly, there are many people who can be classified as the "working poor." They may have a job; however, their job does not pay a high enough wage to cover their basic living expenses. If you pay attention to your work place dynamics, you may discover that one or more of your co-workers face some of these challenges. By being sensitive to these issues, you will have a better understanding of your office environment.

---

2. Help Co-Workers

It is not your responsibility to solve all the problems of your co-workers. However, you should do whatever you can (within reason) to be supportive and helpful to co-workers in need. If you are lucky enough to have a job that you enjoy, then you should be willing to help others enjoy their job. You may provide advice about working with different people, tell others about promotion opportunities, share your secrets of completing work projects sooner, and provide the names of potential mentors. You should simply follow the "Golden Rule" which says: "Treat others as you want to be treated." You should take time to think about the situation other people are in and ask yourself the question: "If I was in that situation, how would I like someone to help me?" The answer to this question will guide your actions.

Some people never help others at work because they view all co-workers as competitors for raises and promotions. They feel that if they help someone, they may be denied an opportunity for advancement. However, frequently, people who are both good at their job and helpful to co-workers are the most likely to get a raise or promotion. These individuals are seen as outstanding team players who usually add significantly more value to the organization than those workers who are singularly focused on their responsibilities. Finally, you never know when you will need help. By helping co-workers, you will earn the respect of your fellow employees and increase the likelihood of receiving help if you ever need it.

---

3. Understand the Problems in Your Community

If you come from a neighborhood with high rates of poverty, you should develop a comprehensive understanding of your community's problems. If you come from a neighborhood with fewer problems, you should identify a community in your area facing many economic challenges and learn as much as you can about the problems in that community. It is easy to leave a poor community when you get a good job and pretend that the community does not exist. It is also easy to grow up in a middle class or rich community and never think about the problems in economically challenged communities. However, the more successful you become, the more important it is for you to understand the problems in poor communities.

If you study the lives of many of the most successful people in the world, you will learn that helping others is one of their major goals in life. They will support or develop programs to help people who are suffering throughout the world. They recognize their responsibility to help to make the world a better place to live in. Even though you may not have achieved great success yet, you should start to think about helping others in need. The best way to do this is to answer five key questions about the poor community that you are focused on helping. These are:

a) What is the poverty rate?
b) What problems are the residents facing?
c) Who are the residents? (What is their background and their family's background?)
d) How can I be most helpful to this community?
e) How can I be most helpful to the people of this community?

---

4. Give Back to Your Community

Once you have answered these five questions, you should develop a comprehensive plan to give back to the community in some way. You may have limited financial resources because you are not earning a high salary. Your time may be limited because of the demands of your job and life. However, you should develop a plan to be helpful to your target community or the people in the community. You may set aside a few hours one weekend a month to read to children who are having trouble in school, you may serve food at a homeless shelter, or you may volunteer your time to work with a local nonprofit organization. You should do something on a regular basis to improve the life of at least one person in that community. Amazingly, you will find that giving back in this way will be one of the most rewarding things that you do in your life.

---

5. Pay Attention to World Problems

Once you have learned about the challenges of people in your target community, you should take the time to learn about the problems of the world. Most people do not take the time necessary to learn about the many problems that people face around the world. They are so focused on their personal problems that they ignore the many (often more significant challenges) that people experience in other countries. Technological advancements have increased our ability to find information about the world around us. We are able to learn more about global problems than ever before. To take advantage of this incredible information, you should force yourself to read the international section of your local newspaper or search the Internet for global news. You will find this information to be both troubling and fascinating. This type of research will give you a deep understanding of the interconnectedness of the world. You will also learn the disturbing reality that many of the world's problems are caused by greed and insensitivity to others. This knowledge will help you be more successful in work and life because it will help you develop a global vision and open your eyes to new career and travel opportunities.

6. Develop an Interest in the Civic Sector

One of the most fascinating things that you will learn about in your global research is the incredible accomplishments of the civic sector. This sector includes relief organizations, social service organizations, education organizations, health care organizations, and other nonprofit organizations around the world that are focused on helping those in need. The nonprofit organizations that comprise the civic sector help the victims of natural disasters, provide health care to individuals suffering from disease, feed the hungry, house the homeless, and educate the illiterate. The civic sector as a whole has the potential to help even more people if it received the political, financial, and volunteer support it needs to address global problems. Unfortunately, world leaders have not embraced this sector in a way that will enable it to address global problems more effectively. Once you learn more about the sector, you will develop a deeper understanding of the importance of the nonprofit organizations in your area.

7. Identify Specific Nonprofits To Support

Your research of global problems and the civic sector may inspire you to learn more about nonprofit organizations in your area. Once you have developed a global perspective, you should spend time researching nonprofit organizations serving communities near your place of work and your home. Find out what services these nonprofits are providing to local communities. Get in contact with many of the leaders of nonprofit organizations to learn more about their mission and operations. Make a special effort to learn as much as you can about the nonprofits that your employer supports (if any). You will probably be very inspired by the good work of the nonprofit organizations in your area. In addition, your research will put you in touch with people in your company and the community who can be helpful to your career aspirations.

8. Volunteer Your Time Regularly

Once you have identified nonprofits to support in your area, you should volunteer to help one or more of these organizations. Most nonprofits are desperately in need of volunteers. They are looking for people to help them operate programs and/or serve on the Board of Trustees. You should review your weekly schedule and determine how much time you have to help your favorite nonprofit organization. If possible, you should schedule your volunteer time in the same way you schedule your other activities. Ideally, you will volunteer at the same place and time every week. You will find that this time is well spent because of the positive emotional stimulation that you will receive from helping others.

9. Give Money

The demands of work and life will prevent you from having as much time as you would like to volunteer for all of your favorite organizations. You should therefore make every effort to contribute money to those organizations that you cannot help as a volunteer. Your contributions can be targeted to support your favorite programs and are generally tax deductible. Nonprofit organizations obviously prefer to get very large donations. However, they appreciate contributions of any size. Do not be embarrassed to contribute a small amount of money. The organizations that are good at fundraising understand the importance of cultivating long-term individual donors because of the potential that one or more of these people will be willing to give a large one-time gift in the future. Your planned regular contribution should be included in your personal budget.

10. Encourage Other People To Give Back

It is wonderful for you to volunteer your time and donate your money to help others. However, you should make every effort to encourage your friends and family to give back to their communities and the world as well. Your generosity should serve as an inspiration to other people to donate their time and money to improve the quality of life of the less fortunate. All too often people are very modest about their efforts to help others. You should feel very comfortable letting your friends and family know how you donate your time and money to help nonprofits who are helping others. Your compassion and willingness to help others will likely inspire your friends and family to follow your lead and either volunteer their time or contribute money to help a good cause. Their concern for the less fortunate will inspire other people to do the same. Before you know, it you will have created a movement dedicated to helping other people. This positive force will help to improve both your quality of life and performance at work because of the intense positive energy that you will receive from inspiring others to give back.

RECOMMENDATION

It is extremely important for you to do what it takes to succeed in work and life. However, that is not enough. You will find that helping other people is more satisfying in the long-run than making a lot of money and having superficial fun. When you improve the quality of life for someone who is suffering, you are helping to make the world a better place to live in. To assess your commitment to helping others, you should complete the following HELPING OTHERS EVALUATION.

HELPING OTHERS EVALUATION

One way to assess how helpful you are to other people is to complete this HELPING OTHERS EVALUATION. Please weight each of the statements below from 5 to 1 and be as honest as you possibly can.

5 = Always
4 = Almost Always
3 = Frequently
2 = Sometimes
1 = Never

A. _____ I pay attention to the challenges people face in my work environment.

B. _____ I help my co-workers.

C. _____ I take time to understand community problems.

D. _____ I give back to my community (or another community in need).

E. _____ I pay attention to world problems.

F. _____ I take time to learn about the civic sector's impact on the world.

G. _____ I have identified one or more nonprofit organizations to support.

H. _____ I volunteer my time regularly.

I. _____ I give money to good causes.

J. _____ I encourage other people to spend their time and money helping others.

By completing this evaluation, you will have a much better idea of the areas that you need to improve to enhance your ability to help others. You should work very hard to improve those areas where you scored a 3 or less. There is nothing like the intense feeling of satisfaction that you get from positively impacting other people and the world. This incredible feeling will probably inspire you to achieve more at work and in life than you ever thought was possible.